# Do Not Go Gentle

# Do Not Go Gentle

Herbert M. Howe

W · W · NORTON & COMPANY · NEW YORK · LONDON

FIRST EDITION

*The text of this book is composed in photocomposition Primer with Corvinus Medium display. Composition and manufacturing are by the Maple-Vail Book Manufacturing Group. Book design by Marjorie J. Flock.*

Library of Congress Cataloging in Publication Data
Howe, Herbert Marshall, 1945–
    Do not go gentle.
    1. Cancer—Biography. 2. Howe, Herbert Marshall,
1945–    3. Athletics—Therapeutic use.
I. Title.
RC263.H68   1981    616.99'4 [B]    80–14732

ISBN 0–393–01390–1

1 2 3 4 5 6 7 8 9 0

DEDICATED to cancer patients with the hope that they may benefit from this book

# Acknowledgments

CHEMOTHERAPY POSSIBLY saved my life, but without friends I could not have endured chemotherapy's pain. *Do Not Go Gentle* mentions many of those who supported me. I particularly wish to single out my parents, the Paysons, and Dr. Loring Conant. I deeply appreciated Judy Athearn, Dr. Lawrence Cloud, Dr. Joel Greenberger, Margaret Handy, Bill Harvey, the staff of Harvard's Health Services, Louise Janowicz, Richard Kessler, Nancy Ott, Dr. Anthony Piro, Dunstan Wai, Sally Weisskopf, Yvonne Quinlan, and, finally, Sylvia Sylvester who as she left life showed others how to live it.

Dianne M. Howser, Leonard Franklin, and Eric Swenson have contributed to the writing of this book as have several cancer specialists. I willingly accept all responsibility for any mistakes while recalling Voltaire's suggestion, "Love truth but pardon error." Finally, I have changed several names and, in a few minor cases, presented composite characters.

# One

"DO THE DOCTORS think that you're going to die?"

I looked at Bill, a fellow teaching assistant at Harvard in African politics. It was a sunny September day in 1976 and we were standing near Harvard's Indoor Athletic Building. A duffel bag under my arm was stuffed with a punching bag and gloves, my swimming trunks, goggles, and a towel. It had been two months since a surgeon had hesitatingly walked to the foot of my hospital bed. He had glanced at me questioningly, then cleared his throat and quietly began.

"Herb, I don't want to shock you but our biopsy shows that you do have cancer, a very rare form of fibrosarcoma. There's an eighty percent chance that you'll die within five years." His announcement rapidly turned my life into an emotional roller coaster as I wrestled with the numerous and complex problems which confront every cancer patient.

Bill was the first person to ask the question so directly. Shrugging my shoulders, I sighed. "The doctors don't know. Most of them are pretty good in admitting that my case baffles them. Fewer than a hundred people in medical history have been discovered with similar symptoms." I grinned. "I guess I'm a bona fide guinea pig."

Bill patted me on the arm and said, "I want you to know

that we're all pulling for you. Don't forget us in the months ahead." Thanking him, I turned and trotted up the steps into the gym.

People often discover their cancer by accident and I was no exception. A ten-year-old relative who kicked a soccer ball at me possibly saved my life. Like too many persons I reacted only when the tumor's size or pain became too obvious to ignore. Cancer's seven warning signals ("change in bowel or bladder habits . . . thickening or lump in breast or elsewhere . . .") were for other, and mostly older, individuals. I would hope my good health could be a self-fulfilling prophecy: wishing would make it so.

Since 1974 I had noticed a small lump on the inside of my right wrist. It was attached to a finger tendon. As I moved a finger up and down, the tumor moved with it. I regarded it as a minor physical aberration. Unless pressure was applied directly, the bump was painless. Twice I passingly mentioned to Harvard's doctors the small bump which occasionally hurt. Inundated by the innumerable ills in which Harvard students indulge, the doctors paid scant attention. "Like everyone else, we deal in probabilities," a Harvard doctor later suggested. "We get hundreds of ganglion cysts but encounter cancer only rarely." Their indifference only confirmed my own lack of interest.

In the spring of 1976 the bump grew more noticeable and susceptible to pain. The turning point for my concern occurred one early July evening in Concord. Close relatives of mine, Smoky and Stephanie Payson, had invited me over for dinner. To clear the house of running feet while Stephanie cooked, I ushered their children into the backyard where we romped about kicking a soccer ball. Harold, at ten the oldest of the three and a good soccer player, suddenly half-spun and ferociously kicked the ball towards me. Instinctively I threw my arm up. The ball slammed against the wrist, soared and landed in a clump of bushes twenty feet away.

As the ball hit me, my knees instantly buckled and pain

seized my entire body. Half-standing I could neither see nor think. Within a few seconds I regained consciousness and slowly raised myself up. Harold trotted over and, concealing his pride in his kick, politely asked if I felt all right. I nodded but, aghast at my body's recent reaction, realized that I would have to discard pride in my body and its presumed infallibility to serious illness. This time I would pressure Harvard to give my wrist more than a cursory examination. The next day the nurse who screens patients to judge whether their complaints merit a doctor's attention suggested that I receive a Novocain injection and come back if the pain persisted. I quietly but firmly refused to leave until a doctor examined me. An hour later a physician gave me the same advice.

Apart from my wrist, the summer of 1976 was proving enjoyable. I was diligently working on my dissertation dealing with the U.S. and the Biafran war. I planned it as a good read; surely it would be the first Harvard dissertation to cite *Dear Abby* ("Tears From Tulsa"), *T.V. Guide,* and *Soldier of Fortune* magazine, as well as such more established sources as Plato, Cicero, and Pliny the Elder. This final year, with its reward of a Ph.D., would justify the past ten years spent in university.

More important, I had just met Claudia, who had just arrived from California. With dark hair, a deep tan, and clear black eyes, Claudia was the most attractive woman I had ever dated. She was intelligent, twenty-two years old, and bubbled with a feisty and optimistic view towards life. Cambridge summers are enjoyable by themselves, but Claudia was making this one especially memorable. Most new relationships strike a magical spark which time eventually snuffs out. Since I didn't know her very well, my infatuation grew each time I saw Claudia. "I feel like I'm eighteen again," I enthused to a friend.

One early afternoon, after having stayed up late with Claudia, I strolled over to Hemenway Gym where I occasionally flailed away at a punching bag. As I walked past the admittance desk, the attendant laughed. "Herb, where'd you get that big grin?" Responding, "Mike, you wouldn't believe this woman," I strolled into the dressing room with thoughts of Claudia on my mind.

As I pummelled the bag in a regular rat-tat-tat staccato beat, I detected a lingering pain whenever my right fist snapped at the bag. I remembered Harold's soccer kick of three weeks before. Under the shower I moved my fingers and gently squeezed the bump. It seemed larger and infinitely more painful than a year ago. No more Novocain and postponements.

The next day, Friday, I saw a Dr. Dunn at the university's health services. As I expressed my concern, he settled back and listened thoughtfully. For once a doctor felt the bump and recorded my pain as he gently pressed his thumb against it.

"It's probably nothing more than a cyst, but I'd like to get you into the hospital. We can operate this Monday." The operation appeared so straightforward and the hospital stay so minimal that I mentioned it to only a few friends.

At the hospital, institutional perplexities soon surfaced. I filled out the same form three times (Height? Six feet, two inches. Age? 31. Hair? Blond.) And, at nine o'clock on Monday morning an officious orderly stopped by my bed and consulted his chart.

"You're going to have to take a shower."

I affably responded, "All right."

"But I see you entered the hospital yesterday and since you have to take a shower every day and since you didn't take one yesterday, you have to take two today."

Could he be serious? "But the operation is in less than two hours. Can't I take one long shower instead?"

"Certainly not." Through his thick glasses he glared at me. "When I come back, both towels had better be wet." His quick departure left no time for my objections, so I ambled to the shower where I dried myself off with one towel and held the other under the shower head. The orderly soon reappeared at my bed. "Rules are rules in a hospital," he intoned as he gingerly picked up two soggy towels. I nodded gravely and he departed.

Soon a nurse sedated me and she was followed by another orderly. Pushing a bed on wheels he instructed me to roll over onto it.

As he fluffed up my pillows I noticed two safety belts. I obligingly reached down and began inserting one end into the other.

"Don't do that, don't ever do that," loudly admonished my chauffeur.

I was stung. "Why not?"

"It's against union policy."

The officiousness of the orderlies and an increasing giddiness from the medication relaxed me. Within such an arena of absurdity one can easily discard usual rationality. I waved to the nurses as I was pushed along innumerable yellow-walled hallways. In the Pre-Op room a walking advertisement for a Dale Carnegie course materialized next to me, pumped my hand, and effusively bubbled, "Hi, there. I'm Mike, your anesthesiologist. I understand you're a Ph.D. from Harvard."

I began to giggle uncontrollably. Finally catching my breath, I quickly rattled off a barrage of Henny Youngman jokes. Dr. Dunn walked in for the last witticism and commented, "It's definitely time to gas him up." A black object moved over my face and I rapidly faded from consciousness.

Several hours later the increasing pain from the incision and the lessening power of the anesthetic temporarily woke me. Woozily, I noticed two surgeons hovering over me.

"What did you find?" I weakly inquired. I thought I heard the female doctor reply, "We thought it was only a cyst but now we think it may be cancer. We're having tests to make sure." I drifted back to sleep.

Later that evening in the hospital room I woke up. At

first I had no idea of where I was or what I was doing. Then I noticed my arm encased in a cast and suspended from a rod above me. A crucifixion image drifted through my groggy brain. My arm hurt, my mouth was desperately dry, and my head throbbed with a pulsating ache. The room was dark and quiet and I grew very nervous.

What did that doctor say? Am I crazy or did she say cancer? But it was only supposed to be a cyst. I racked my memory, trying to decide whether I had only dreamt the scene in the Post-Op room.

I re-ran the scene of her looking down at me and saying, "It may be cancer." The scene became increasingly more real as I recalled additional details. Alone at four in the morning, weak, and still aching from pain, I was now convinced that I might have cancer. Just before daybreak I dozed off for a few restless hours.

Greasy bacon, soggy toast, and cold pancakes. I shoved aside the breakfast tray and asked the nurses if they knew the results of my operation. Negative. Could they find out? They promised to check.

I remember Tuesday largely as a day of pain. The swelling, or edema, was squeezing the incision against the cast. With other operations the pain had slackened by the second day; this time it was increasing. I would have felt peppier if I had slept the previous two nights. But my apprehensions received no rest from hospital routine: the intercom's incessant paging, groans and wailings from unseen patients, and nurses with their flashlights drifting like fireflies through the dark. I felt ignored and helpless, desperately wishing to leave the hospital.

I could have helped the situation by having friends visit me. Yet I considered such a request as an unnecessary inconvenience for them. The hospital was not well-connected to mass transit and I assumed that I would return to Harvard within a few days. So, I quietly lay in my bed and allowed worries to give birth to more worries. I thought of Dunn and the woman doctor and their subsequent silence and remembered a line from Robert Frost. "We dance round in a ring and suppose, But the Secret sits in the middle and knows."

In the late afternoon the floor doctor kindly lowered my cast from the suspending rod. He smiled and asked if I needed anything else.

"Do I have cancer?" I responded.

He blanched and inquired why I had asked. He listened to my recollection of the Post-Op room and suggested that I had been heavily drugged. I shrugged and asked him to inquire about my situation. Neither he nor the nurses reported back.

By seven in the evening I was desperate to confide my fears to a friend. After the nurses had cleared the trays, filled the water glasses, and then left, I slowly slid my feet off the bed's edge and onto the floor.

"Hey, man, where you goin'? You can't do that!" The room's other occupant, an elderly black man, glanced at me.

"The hell I can't," I rejoined. He chuckled and watched as I searched my pants for a dime. Craning my neck out the door I ascertained that the coast was clear. Bracing myself against the wall for support and keeping my right arm raised, I struggled to the phone booth. It was an interminable walk of sixty feet.

I dropped the dime into the phone and called Claudia. The small booth reeked with the vile smell of forty years of sweat, cigarettes, and cigars. I kept peering to make sure no white-frocked sentry was patrolling. Claudia's phone kept ringing. A nurse was walking towards me. Damn. I twisted my body so she would not notice the arm. I felt nauseated from the cigarettes. Hurry up, Claud.

"Hello." Finally.

Before telling her the news of possible cancer I perfunctorily asked how she was doing. Hesitatingly, she replied.

"Herb, I've been thinking a lot about returning to California. I really miss my close friends and I think I'll enroll in Japanese art at Seattle for the fall semester. I'll miss you but I'm sure it's the right thing. By the way, where are you?"

I was stunned. Now that she was leaving I could not tell her about the cancer. Unthinking, I sat in the telephone booth for ten minutes. I shuffled back to my bed where glowering nurses reprimanded me for my unauthorized stroll. Swallowing sleeping pills, I plunged into a fitful, tossing, and largely sleepless night.

I was transferred to a private room at Harvard's infirmary late Wednesday afternoon. As the rising sun slowly changed my dark curtains to a fiery crimson, I realized that another night and the chance for sleep had vanished. Tears streamed down my face. Increasing pain from the edema and my frustration about not being told about the operation's results were taking their toll. Up and down my right arm, pain ran a frantic pattern. I grabbed a small notebook and squeezed it in my right hand. Nobody was going to see me cry. My left arm tried to wipe away the continuing tears. I must have looked a mess.

A black woman orderly walked in holding a huge pile of bed linen. She glanced sidewards at me. "You're in a whole lot of pain, aren't you, Mr. Howe?" I grudgingly nodded and involuntarily began sobbing. She threw down the linen and ran out the door. In a few minutes a nurse, a doctor, and, surprisingly, the director of Harvard's health services were standing by my bed.

"I can't sleep. I don't know what's wrong with me and my wrist hurts like hell. Please take the cast off and what's my prognosis?"

"But it's normal," the director countered, "to have pain after an operation. You'll soon be better."

I beseechingly looked at him. "I've had six other operations and nothing has ever hurt like this."

They bustled off to consult with my surgeon. "Dr. Dunn says that the cast can come off and we'll give you a pain pill."

"What's my prognosis?"

"Dr. Dunn says that he'll try to see you soon."

Another delay. Why? And why this private room and the appearance by the director of health services?

As a doctor sliced the cast off my wrist I felt a surge of exquisite pleasure scamper up my arm. I thanked him while a nurse gave me a pain pill.

Just before falling asleep I recall a massive grin spreading across my face. For the next three hours I watched a single, three-dimensional scene. A small, perhaps six-year-old, blonde girl in a yellow pinafore roamed the top of a hill picking yellow daffodils. I was part of the scene, although the girl never noticed me. White butterflies fluttered before the light blue sky. I could smell the rich dark soil and feel the thick wet grass topped with dew. It was a scene of innocence and contentment.

Shortly after noon, a knock upon the door dissipated my illusion. "Mr. Howe, you're certainly smiling now," noted the woman orderly. I laughed and expressed my appreciation for her recent aid. I refrained from complimenting the staff on their pain pills.

I urgently felt the need for my close friends. Since I was now at Harvard, inconvenience to their schedules would be minimal. While I did not want the large dollops of sympathy served to patients, I actually looked forward to the usual clumsy hospital jokes and aimless talk.

In the late afternoon Claudia dropped by. She smiled as I apologized for not having combed my hair or shaved. "Don't be silly," she suggested while stuffing some daisies into a water pitcher and then passing me a pint of chocolate ice cream. "I wanted to see you, so let's forget about appearances." She sat on the bed and we began spooning the rapidly melting ice cream.

But the conversation soon grew painful. After mentioning her reasons for returning to California, she concluded that while she strongly liked me, I appeared, among other things, to be unnecessarily glib.

"It wasn't the only time but when you called from the hospital, you just didn't tell me why you were there or how you were doing. Just some stories about orderlies and bad jokes."

I struggled against telling her my fears about having cancer. "It's not fair," I thought. "She's leaving, and telling her now would only make her feel helpless and guilty about leaving." It was only a cyst, I informed her. We vowed to see each other soon but as she left I could not help feeling that somebody I needed very much would soon be out of my life.

That evening I understood the value of friends. At six, Baruch and Stewie bounced into the room. Grinning surreptitiously they pulled from a knapsack two six-packs of Heineken.

"Not now." I reluctantly turned down a drink. "The doctor's on his rounds and will be here soon." When the doctor did appear I asked him about my condition and he claimed that he had not seen my chart.

I grew morose, wondering why no doctor seemed to have faith in my ability to handle bad news. "What's the matter?" asked Baruch as he emptied his second bottle. I mentioned my fears of cancer. "Oh, Jesus, you really do need this," he ordained as he planted a full six-pack on my bed.

Agreeing, I started drinking and waving greetings to other friends as they paraded into the room, greeted with loud cheers from Baruch and Stewie. Debby, a close buxom friend of mine was awarded the only chair while everyone else sat on the floor, backs against the wall. A total of ten people had brought seven six-packs.

The noise level rose constantly. As Debby rhetorically shouted, "Is it okay to drink in a hospital?" a nurse suddenly walked in to take my pulse. Her gaze began with the cavorters upon the floor and proceeded to the bed's occupant who was frantically wondering how to transform a green Heineken's bottle into a glass of orange juice.

Rolling her eyes upward, the intruder remarked, "You know, it's much too early for all this." Spurning all offers that she stop her work early that night, she took my pulse and exited. Boos, cheers, and assorted commentaries upon the nursing profession followed her down the hall.

I lay back contentedly and gazed at my friends. My hesitancy about imposing upon them had been totally unfounded; everyone was enjoying themselves. For the first time since the operation I felt totally relaxed.

When someone exhibited unmitigated nerve by asking why I had been operated on, a now totally drunk Baruch offered a John Wayne intonation. "The kid's got cancer and he's going to die. So there." The room exploded with guffaws and drawn out giggles. An embarrassing moment had been sidestepped.

At nine, the intercom announced that visiting hours were over. All alone, I elected to walk to the TV room and watch the end of the Red Sox game. Afterwards, to get back to my room I had to walk past the nurses' station. I suddenly felt very vulnerable. The much too short hospital johnnie was insecurely tied in the back. I was fairly drunk, tired, and dejected about my unrevealed medical status.

As I quietly shuffled barefooted past the station the head nurse, an imposing grande dame, leaned over her desk. Stiffly pointing her finger at me she queried, "And how many beers did *you* have, Mr. Howe?"

I gulped. In searching for a reply I realized that, since she knew about the party, protestations of innocence were futile. Better minimize it, I decided. I opened my mouth to say "one." Instead, a horrendously loud belch followed. The nurse with arm extended froze, while her junior nurses doubled over with laughter. Herb, now you've really blown it. They'll kick you out. Worrying that my johnnie might completely disassemble, I scurried to my room, undoubtedly pursued by the reproachful glare of the senior nurse.

An hour later Smoky called. He and Stephanie along with my sister, brother-in-law, and six assorted nieces and nephews were travelling the next day to his parents in Bristol, Rhode Island. Scampering around Narragansett Bay with gap-toothed children would be the perfect antidote for my present worry and passivity. The doctor who had seen me earlier that evening had told me that I could leave on Saturday. I jumped at the offer and Smoky promised to call me early Saturday morning.

With the cast off and an anticipated trip, I managed a few hours of sleep and ate most of my breakfast. I joked about the previous night with the nurses and orderlies. "I mean, it has to be against rules—hell, I thought that old nurse would send me packing." My respect for the nursing profession soared when I was told that, while the liquor was not quite what the doctor had ordered ("he'd consider all the medication you've taken"), the nurses realized that relaxation with friends was what I needed most after the pain and sleepless nights. In the ensuing three years, my admiration for nurses has generally increased. Their pragmatic judgment and consideration for their patients has enabled them to adapt hospital doctrine to human needs.

Saturday morning presented Cambridge with a familiar weather pattern: dark gray overcast with steady rain expected to last through the weekend. Inside the infirmary I fidgeted as nurses sought permissions and signatures for my checkout.

I was lifting myself from the bed when the voice over the intercom announced, "Smoky Payson wishes to talk to you."

At that exact same moment Dr. Dunn hurried into the room and shouted back, "Tell him Howe will call back later."

I blinked. Dunn appeared nervous, distraught, yet extraordinarily intent upon delivering a message to me. I moved up in my bed, rested my head on the clump of pillows, and focused upon Dunn.

"You're going off somewhere?"

"Smoky and some other relatives of mine are driving to Rhode Island today and I'm joining them."

Dunn considered this. "All right."

He paused and looked about my private room: his reflection in the mirror, the always immaculate sink, and the large picture window displaying the rain, grayness, and grubby red brick of Harvard. He studied the floor, shuffled his feet, and began talking.

"We didn't tell you the surgical results because we were surprised by what we found. There was no cyst. There was a tumor and we had to determine its malignancy. I was very cautious because while I thought it was cancer I had never seen anything like it."

"Is it cancer?"

"Yes."

"How bad is it?"

"I don't want to shock you but I think you should reevaluate your goals in life. It's a very rare form of fibrosarcoma. In medical history fewer than a hundred people have had it. There's an eighty percent probability of your dying within five years."

Like any good graduate student confronted with new information I began to take notes. Dunn glanced at me and continued.

"I realize this is very sudden, that it's a powerful blow. You may go into shock later today when you've given it more thought. But it's not necessarily lethal and if you make it past five years then you're in the clear."

Not necessarily lethal. Small consolation. Yet I smiled tightly for somehow I figured that there would be no shock. I was relieved to have my worst fears confirmed. Now I knew my position. I scanned my notes, "Not necessarily lethal." "Muscle cancer." "Eighty percent." I asked what I could do.

"I'll let you leave today but I want to see you in ten days to remove the sutures. By then, specialists will have examined the slides and we can be more specific about prognosis and treatment. Anything else?"

Anything else? Am I going to die, what about raising a family, whom do I tell, what about insurance, school, future jobs ("I want the job but I must tell you that I have cancer")?

But I shook my head and looked back at him. Dunn appeared relieved that the session was over. In an even voice he expressed sadness about bearing the bad news and that he looked forward to seeing me soon. He then turned and walked out the door.

Perhaps I should have lain on my bed for the next few hours and reflected upon the significance of Dunn's announcement, but immediate needs offered themselves as welcome distractions. I journeyed to the bathroom. Soon afterwards I was awkwardly pulling on a pair of blue jeans and then trying to button my shirt with one hand.

Smoky must have been wondering why he was cut off. I called and he answered on the first ring.

"Herb, what's happening down there?"

I quickly and firmly decided that I would be honest with Smoky. The doctors' vagueness about my operation still piqued me.

"Smoky, I've got cancer and there's an eighty percent chance of dying within five years."

He gently reprimanded me, "Herb, you're kidding."

"I never would kid about this, Smoky."

A long pause. "I guess you're right, Herb. Oh gosh, I'm sorry. I really don't know what to say." Lin, my sister, was in the room with Smoky. She recalls, "I was lying on the sofa and when Smoky suddenly became serious, I sat up. 'My God, this is my brother and he's got cancer.' "

Smoky presented long-term questions and condolences but my voice was cracking. I felt tears welling up. Interrupting a question, I told him and Lin to meet me outside Elsie's Delicatessen in half an hour.

Packing my suitcase I thought, "I've got cancer and I'm leaving to visit the ocean." The whole week had become an uncontrollable absurdity.

At the checkout desk a nurse asked me perfunctory questions while averting her eyes from me. I asked, "Have the doctors told you what's wrong with me?" She didn't answer but began to walk down the hall. "Have they?" She stopped for a second, looked over her shoulder and in a breaking voice said, "No."

Outside it was still drizzling. As I stood holding a suitcase in my left hand I wondered how Lin and Smoky were reacting. I did not know that Lin had spent a sleepless night in the Albany bus station ("very skillfully designed," she commented, "to make it impossible for anyone to fall asleep. I suppose it keeps the tramps out") and had one hour of sleep before hearing of her brother's diagnosis and leaving for Elsie's. "As we drove through the rain to get you," she recalled, "I was in a strange limbo. I understood you had cancer, but could only wonder what the dirty rain of Cambridge would do to the nice clean bandages on your wrist."

As Smoky's VW stationwagon drew up, he and Lin jumped out and the three of us stood awkwardly in the rain. When Lin finally said, "We'd better get going," we quietly climbed into the car. Smoky was driving us to the bus station. He and Stephanie would drive down later with their children.

The flood of questions rose as the bus sped towards Rhode Island. Do I tell my sister's in-laws, the Paysons (who also were old family friends)? While I did not consider them especially close, I felt qualms at arriving as an unannounced houseguest who proceeds to dump his medical laundry in their laps. Yet they were mature and caring adults who could discuss my predicament with perhaps a valuable detachment.

What about my various nephews and nieces, the oldest of whom was entering the sixth grade? I told Lin, "I've always thought adults repressed the facts of death from children. I'm willing to tell them. I'd be equally willing to see them less and less, cutting the emotional attachment between us. I'll do what you want."

Lin considered this. "Let's not be hasty and do some-

thing we later might regret. We'll treat it as a normal oper
tion for now. And don't detach yourself from them. You'
something special to them; they'd be hurt."

Should I tell my parents now or wait several days un
more doctors examined the biopsy? Perhaps I should te
them that it was a tumor and that no one was yet su
whether it was benign or malignant. Both of us quick
agreed that any repression would make me feel guilty ar
worry them needlessly with unanswered questions.

As the bus swept down the rain-slickened highway
reflected that it was grossly unfair that without any war
ing or preparation I had to make innumerable decisior
which would not only affect me but practically everyone
knew.

Yet a sense of adventure was equally present. Mo
than any other disease, cancer has a certain romance ar
challenge attached to it. Remembrances from *Death I
Not Proud* and *Brian's Song*. I suddenly felt important ar
less acquiescent to other peoples' opinions. Never did
consider suicide; life had suddenly become too exciting.

In Providence I first noticed this new assertivenes
Switching buses for Bristol, we groaned when we saw
long queue for tickets. I told Lin to lug the bags to the Bri
tol bus. With only three minutes before the bus left, I ran
the front of the line. Two statuesque and very proper dow
gers with flowered hats stood in front.

"Excuse me," I blurted, "but I've got fatal cancer ar
have to catch a bus." Either out of concern or befuddl
ment they stepped back and let me pass. Cancer, I began
realize, could give me a certain power. I was allowed to ta
chances and break rules.

I told my Bristol relatives. They quickly concurred tha
should tell my parents but not mention the word cancer
my nieces and nephews: "It's a scare word and most u
necessary for them."

This was a fortunate decision. All six children helpe
me enormously during that gray, wet weekend. We held i
numerable races down the hill to the harbor. Giggling a

the way, we collapsed in the sand at the finish line. Hide-and-go-seek, Frisbee games, and even strolls along the beach lent a much needed frivolity to the situation for as I grew physically exhausted I felt the tension drain away. Unknowingly, the children symbolized a certain optimistic naïveté into which I could retreat and burrow until faced with adults and the realization that I had an illness which would not go away. If I had told the kids about my cancer, the week would have been unnecessarily grim.

Saturday's dinner began quietly and awkwardly. The senior Mrs. Payson tried to compensate for our quiet by urging her cooking upon all of us. I appreciated having relatives around me but could not interest myself in their desultory conjectures and complaints about the continuing rain. I needed to discuss cancer but hesitated to push it as a topic.

Smoky had been watching me intently and finally broke a long silence.

"The doctors give you an eighty percent chance of dying. How are you taking it?"

"It's the uncertainty that bothers me," I quickly replied. "I'm not sure what I'm up against. More important, I don't know what I can do."

Smoky thought for a moment. "You've always enjoyed athletics. I wonder if vigorous exercise could somehow help you."

I shrugged and said nothing. To myself I thought, sports probably can't cure cancer but it wouldn't be a bad way to die. Smoky then queried me about what I would do if, hypothetically, I knew that I was going to die within the year. I offered some hesitant suggestions and then everyone except the children, who were ensconced in the living room, entered into the conversation.

Tension disappeared as we all expressed various fears and hopes. It would be incumbent upon me, I realized, to be candid and open when discussing cancer. People seemed to be less afraid of cancer than of speaking about it.

The conversation stretched far past the meal. As the

elder Mrs. Payson cleared away the dishes, her husband, a retired Navy captain, glanced inquiringly at me.

"Perhaps you should call your parents now."

A knot tightened in my stomach. I could handle the cancer better than I could inform my friends about it. I had received Dunn's announcement with aplomb but had experienced great difficulty when talking over the phone to Smoky.

I called Madison, Wisconsin every half hour until midnight. No answer. It was incredible; hardly ever did they stay out after nine. Had something happened to them? I called my younger sister in Wisconsin. No response.

As the tension built within me I walked down to the bay and to the end of the Payson's pier. Somewhere off in the dark a few lights twinkled and occasionally a foghorn cut its way through the quiet night. A thick fog began to wrap itself around me. I turned and walked back slowly to the house. Everyone had retired. I turned off all the lights and climbed softly up the stairs.

Other cancer patients agree that the first night after the announcement constitutes one of the most difficult periods of adjustment. Without any diversions or family support I found myself grappling with painful and unanswerable questions. Why me; why do young people have to get it; what caused it; what can I do about it; will I die; how may I plan ahead when I might die within the year?

As my right arm hung over the side of the bed I felt the incision pulse with the flow of blood. As tears streamed down my face I seriously allowed my disease to assume a demonic personality—an evil predator growing uncontrollably within me, ingesting my healthy cells. I pictured it as a large and confident snake grinning broadly.

My lower arm began to twitch. I sobbed uncontrollably. The wrist was still twitching when I fell asleep at four thirty.

By noon on Sunday I felt calmer, drained of most emotion. Blithefully unaware of my illness, the children continually scampered through the seventeen-room house and shrieked at practical jokes they played on each other. Parents and grandparents fumed, screamed, and pleaded with them to simmer down. I sat back and warmed to their actions, so free of thought.

Outside, the rain kept pouring. Eventually I grew restless. I slipped unnoticed from the living room and pulled on an old raincoat. Through the rain I walked down Hope Street.

Since my father had been born and raised in Bristol, my family often visited the town as I was growing up and I had warm memories of Bristol. I walked past the Herreshoff piers, where all the America's Cup boats between 1893 and 1930 had been built. As a youngster I had darted between the docks and dreamt of sailing on the sleek boats cutting through Narragansett Bay. Outside the nearby Lobster Pot I remembered being ten years old and gobbling a whole lobster as melted butter flowed down my chin. Slightly further on, my grandfather's house jutted onto the Bay. Hurricane Carol had unexpectedly lashed Bristol in the summer of 1954 and, being only nine years old, I had delighted in the storm. When banished to a safe room, I had curled up with my grandfather's cocker spaniel and contentedly read Hardy Boy mysteries.

But these memories were from my youth, when I thought I would live forever. Turning, I trudged back to the Paysons.

The children were still scampering about when I returned. Mrs. Payson seized upon me to serve dinner to the kids while the other adults ate in the dining room.

As the children's energy slumped, the tension rose again within me. I could not reach my parents or younger sister in Wisconsin. In preparation I had instructed Lin to stand closeby when I called, in case I could not complete the call. Finally, at eleven at night, my father picked up the phone.

"Dad, it's me. Do you remember I was in the hospital last week for an operation?"

"What happened?"

"The results have turned out badly. While tentative, they apparently show that I've got a very serious form of cancer. Fewer than a hundred people in medical history have had it."

"But what are your chances?"

"They're really quite unsure, perhaps a twenty to thirty percent survival chance. But the doctors are uncertain and will know a lot more when I get back at the end of the week."

A long silence. "Well, you know that we'll always stand by you."

"Yes, I realize that and thanks a lot." Relieved that I had completed my duty I transferred the phone to my sister who more fully recounted the recent events.

For the next few days I soared and plummeted on an emotional roller coaster. On Monday a hurricane quickly moved up from the Carolinas. "I'd like to stay. It'll be an excellent diversion. Anyways, I can help out even with one arm." My pleas fell upon deaf ears and I was driven back to Massachusetts.

After my first day back in Cambridge I called up an acquaintance, the nutritionist Jean Mayer. "I think I can handle what the disease might be doing to me, Dr. Mayer. But I need advice on how to tell other people. Today one friend said, 'I wish you hadn't told me' while another friend got angry when I didn't tell her." Mayer strongly recommended that I talk to Dr. Loring Conant at Harvard. Mayer's advice would prove to be excellent.

I arranged to meet with Conant on Thursday afternoon. That morning I visited a nurse in Harvard's physical therapy room.

"Nancy, I'd like to know about fibrosarcoma." She gestured towards a thick red book. On page 377 I read that "for fibrosarcoma in the extremities (hands and feet) amputation is usually the preferred remedy." Even more than death, I had always feared the loss of an arm or leg. Now, that morbid fear could be real. I slumped forward, stunned.

Just before I left to see Conant, my advisor called from his vacation home in Maine. "Herb, there's a vacancy for a government professor at the University of Maine. It's yours for the asking." After hanging up the phone, I shouted triumphantly and ran up and down the hall. Life wasn't so bad, after all.

I had known Conant casually as a fellow member of Dudley House's Senior Common Room. The Senior Common Room is a delightful institution; its main purpose is to bring faculty and selected students together for a formal lunch each Wednesday. Over food and wine, students and teachers trade jokes, attempted witticisms, and philosophical discursions on the Boston Red Sox. The Senior Common Rooms at Harvard have probably broken down more barriers between teacher and student than a bundle of formal, well-intentioned committees.

As I entered Conant's office he rose to greet me. A boyish looking thirty-seven, he extended his hand and gently asked me to sit down. Mayer had already called him and explained the situation. Conant listened to my problems for a while and then interrupted me. "Herb, before I try to advise you on how to discuss your cancer with other people, let me find out if the Tumor Board* has discussed your case."

As Conant called, I realized that he was getting fairly conclusive evidence as to whether I would live or die. But perhaps because of the Maine teaching position or because I realized I could do nothing to affect the verdict, I sat back and thought about that night's date with Claudia and my upcoming visit to Madison.

At length Conant put the phone down and turned to me. "I've got great news. You have excellent chances for complete recovery." He anticipated my question. "By 'excellent' I mean between ninety and a hundred percent

---

* A weekly meeting of Boston's top cancer specialists where they discuss unusual cases.

chance. For added assurance, you'll have radiation ther-
apy."

We talked for a short while and then I rose to leave.
Conant's last words to me were "You've been through a
storm but it's blown over. Fortunately, there's nothing to
worry about." I had to agree. Six days ago I assumed that I
would die shortly. Now, not only was I going to live but I
had a highly desirable job. I had rediscovered my need for
friends in difficult times as well as their enthusiasm to
respond. A difficult challenge had come and gone and it
had not bowled me over.

As I left Conant's office I was filled with pride and a
sense of accomplishment. It had been a fascinating six
days and now I could return to normal. As later events
proved, however, the next few weeks would only be the
lull.

Over the next eight months I would experience photon
and neutron radiation sessions, psychiatric consultations,
and chemotherapy treatments (which the late Senator
Humphrey called "bottled death"). I would somehow en-
dure a physical and near nervous breakdown as well as
temporary baldness and an extended period of asexuality.
And I grew very scared of death, of life's finiteness (or what
Gail Sheehy concisely calls "the arithmetic of life").

The real storm had not yet begun.

# Two

A WEEK LATER I was lying on the hot sand of Provincetown, blissfully letting the water surge up my legs and then languidly trickle down. A few days after Conant had told me of the Tumor Board's reassessment, I had driven to Provincetown for a final summer vacation with Debby and other Dudley House students.

As I lay on the beach I thought of the operation's aftermath and of telling friends about my cancer. As I called my parents after talking with Conant about the Tumor Board, I imagined them standing by the phone. My mother is five feet tall, and has gray hair and a crisp English accent. My father stands more than a foot taller and is remarkably trim, a result of the two miles which he swims every day.

My mother listened quietly to the update, said, "Well, thank God," and then passed the phone to my father. He was delighted when he heard the Board's findings. He then proceeded to tell me about "other Howes who have had some strange crossings with death."

My father has an understandable pride in the historical variety of the Howe family. My ancestors and relations include Mayflower passengers, Revolutionary War soldiers, inventors, horse thieves, a Harvard president, slave traders, and a winner of the Pulitzer prize. However, I questioned

the need for a long distance call to retrace an already famil-
iar past. Equally, however, my father was not to be denied.

"Abigail, who was your great, great, grandmother," he
began, "had three sons who served on the crew of one of
her husband's ships trafficking between Massachusetts
and China. In the middle of a ferocious evening snowstorm
in 1801, Abigail awoke suddenly and cried out, 'The boys!
They're dead!' There was a clap of thunder and a table in
her room jumped up and turned upside down. Everyone at
breakfast thought that poor Abigail had suffered a bad
nightmare. Two days later a boat sailed into Bristol harbor
with the news that the snowstorm had sunk her husband's
boat off Cape Cod. The waves had washed onto the shore-
line the bodies of her three dead sons."

Before he got off another example I asked "Dad, has
cancer run in our family?"

My father's Rolodex mind flipped through the possibil-
ities. "Yes, by God, your great Uncle Arthur. When he was
in his seventies, he developed cancer of the vocal cords. Ev-
eryone expected him to die that same year—1936. But in a
hoarse whisper that November he announced that he
wouldn't die until a Republican entered the White House.
He got back all his vigor and didn't die until he was ninety-
four, soon after Ike was elected. Your mother knows of no
one in her family. Except, of course, you."

The reactions of my friends varied widely. Tony ques-
tioned whether I had been responsible for my cancer. Cit-
ing arguments by Wilhelm Reich, he questioned whether I
had traditionally repressed my personal feelings and
whether I had difficulty in developing close relationships. I
was annoyed by Tony's questions. It was bad enough hav-
ing cancer. It was worse being blamed for it.

A married couple viewed my cancer as somehow im-
moral and possibly contagious. "They think I've got a social
disease," I mentioned to an amused Debby. When I first
told Sandy of my operation, she glanced hesitantly at my
swollen incision, which strikingly resembled a bloated,
purplish worm. "Yeeech," she screamed and jerked away.

Ryan simply shook his head and said, "I really wish you hadn't told me." Ryan and Sandy would wait six months before calling me on the phone.

I was surprised that learning about my cancer was easier than telling friends about it. Practice did not make perfect; who to tell, when, how, and exactly how much to tell were questions that I had to resolve individually with each friend. I instinctively shied away from hurting friends and, after Ryan and Sandy, feared being rejected. Also, the pity that usually followed my announcement made me uncomfortable.

One very close friend, upon hearing the news, suddenly reached into his pocket and extracted a five dollar bill.

"You, you never know when y-y-you'll need this now," he stammered.

Stunned, I finally replied, "Christ, I sure don't need this." If I still had cancer, I would need all the self-esteem I could muster. While the offer insulted me, implying that I was no longer able to care for myself, I grudgingly realized that I had once felt the same way about ill people.

Fortunately, my encounter with cancer brought some people closer to me. Living in the same house, Jane Lesley and I had gotten along well, albeit superficially. And it was Jane who had introduced me to Claudia. Yet I felt that I didn't know her well enough to mention my cancer.

One sunny afternoon I was sitting alone in Dudley's dining room when Jane sat down and immediately asked about the operation's results. Reluctantly I told her. Jane paled and swallowed hard. "Oh shit, I've blown it again," I thought to myself.

As I learned later, Jane had rarely thought of cancer, assuming "that it struck only children or aging adults." But two months before my operation, her younger sister had contracted Hodgkin's. Then, two hours before seeing me in Dudley, she had met her best friend, Miriam, for lunch. Miriam had just returned from her doctor, who had informed her that she had breast cancer.

"I was totally crushed as I listened to you," remembers

Jane. "Suddenly cancer was hitting home. It seemed to be attacking everybody at once. We all seemed so vulnerable and, of course, I wondered about myself. I remember looking at you and thinking 'First my kid sister, then Miriam, then you. Am I next?' "

Jane shook her head in disbelief as I finished describing the operation and the differing prognoses. Then she reached across the table and grasped my good arm. "If you ever, and I *mean* ever, need my help, you just call." Over the next year Jane became one of my dearest friends, always treating me with a correct balance of concern and irreverent humor.

Finally, my operation had one good effect. When I visited Dunn to have my sutures removed, he grabbed my left arm and saying, "feel this," directed it to his stomach. There, to my surprise, was a golfball-sized lump. I glanced up at him for an explanation.

"I've had it for at least five years," Dunn smiled self-deprecatingly, "and never really thought twice about it. I must've thought it was a harmless cyst. But as I opened you up I was thinking 'Howe's got a cyst like mine.' When I saw that your 'cyst' was cancer I asked myself, 'Hey, what do I have?' " Dunn seemed to smile gratefully at me. "I'm having it removed tomorrow," he said.

Lying on the Provincetown beach I increasingly found myself thinking about Claudia. Claudia, more than cancer or death. Before driving to Provincetown I had mentioned to her that the doctors had discovered and then removed a cancerous tumor and that I had nothing to worry about. She wanted to know more but I had immediately switched to another topic. I kept thinking about Claudia; I called her the next morning.

"Claud, I'm leaving tomorrow for Madison and you'll have left by the time I get back. I'd like to see you tonight."

"You're leaving tomorrow?"

"That's right."

Following a long silence, Claudia said that she had

been thinking about us a lot and, yes, she wanted to see me.

The wind was blowing, an early hint of fall, as I drove through the twilight out to West Newton. Impatiently waiting at a red light, I was surprised by my nervous energy. I felt as if I was back in the tenth grade, nervously anticipating my first date ever with Polly Eberhardt.

Why did I want to see Claudia again? I certainly didn't want any pity. While I wanted to wrap up a pleasant relationship, I hoped to understand how she could have affected me so deeply in such a short time.

Claudia escorted me into the bright butcherblock kitchen. Her glistening black hair and California tan contrasted sharply with her white blouse.

I plopped the grocery bag onto a countertop and watched salad trappings spill out. Claudia, with arms folded, was studying me intently as she leaned against the refrigerator. "If she's moody tonight," I thought, "it won't help me much." Striving for some levity I picked up a Hostess Sno-Ball, which is really a man-made pink sponge, and joked that Claudia's nutritionist mother would disown her for eating such junk food.

Claudia tightened perceptibly and said nothing. Finally forcing a weak smile she asked, "Herb, what do the doctors think?"

I had prepared myself for such questions. I breezily replied, "There's no question but that I've got a long and profitable life ahead." Suggesting that there was nothing to worry about, I asked her about her Washington plans.

Claudia had not budged. Now she unfolded her arms and walked uncertainly toward me while I nervously shifted my weight.

"Damn it, Herb. This isn't very easy on me. I've been attracted to you, but frustrated that I've never understood you. And now I'm leaving." Shaking her head emphatically she said, "Well, tonight I'm not going to stand for any of your usual glibness."

She had liked me after the first week, but had been angered that I tended to see her as a stereotype. "For example, you didn't really know me but you assumed that I was a woman who only majored in art history as an excuse to go to college. Not only was that arrogant, but coming from a Harvard Ph.D. it was also intimidating." Claudia scrutinized me. "I wonder about you a lot," she said. "After all, you're a grown man and probably can't change much anymore."

Claudia cut off my response. "I really wrestled with seeing you tonight. I've always felt uncomfortable in front of ill people. But okay, I'm here and I'm not going to nod like a fuckin' marionette at your banalities." Hesitating for a moment Claudia threw up her hands. "Herb, I'm sorry," she signed. "I guess I'm still angry about your not telling me about the cancer and, even now just brushing it off as nothing." She looked intently at me and lowered her voice. "Herb, it's our last night. Let's be honest. I think it would help both of us."

As we stood in the middle of the kitchen looking at each other I remember thinking that Claudia bore an uncanny resemblance to Linda Ronstadt on the cover of "Hasten down the Wind." Claudia ran her hands through her wedge-styled hair and peered at me questioningly. I felt as if I were still with Polly Eberhardt and wondering what she would do if I kissed her. I looked again at Claudia. "Does she really want to hear my feelings?" I asked myself.

I finally mentioned that the six days had been difficult, having not only to deal with cancer but how to tell relatives and friends. "I didn't tell you right away because you were going home and so why should I load you with some extra hassle?" Claudia studied me, then nodded and began to set the table.

Two hours later we were still lingering over dinner, all previous reluctance having melted away as, like relaxed confidants, we discussed what we wanted in a relationship while joking about our initial perceptions of each other. No need for pretense existed: this was our last night together.

In the living room several framed family portraits lay propped against the wall; tomorrow Claudia's relatives would be moving into their new home. A particularly dour ancestor, a witness to this evening from an early, more puritanical period, glared at us. "You don't have to worry," I silently assured him. I thought back to our first night together. I had been sitting in a chair by Claudia's bed as she entered the room dressed in a flannel nightgown. After chatting for several minutes Claudia, now reclining on her queensize bed, studied me and smiled impishly. "California men," she observed, "are not as formal." My irresolutions had exited abruptly. But tonight I wanted to talk with her: going to bed would seem mechanical, a waste of time.

As the grandfather clock struck nine, Claudia removed the dinner plates and placed cheese and crackers on the table. She cupped a cracker in her palm, spread some cheese, and passed it to me.

"After you first told me about your cancer, I thought about something that once happened to me." Her voice trailed off and she looked uncertainly at me. I nodded and she studied her wine. "I haven't told this to many people, Herb," she said slowly, "but, well, when I heard about your cancer, I immediately thought about me and my dad."

Her father had been an alcoholic. When Claudia was in grade school, life had proven an ongoing exercise in anger, frustration, and temporary forgivings. Finally her mother had enough. She gathered her children and stormed from the house.

"Dad suddenly got really angry. He shouted at us to stay. But Mom said, 'I've got five children and leaving you means that they'll survive.' For the next few years I really missed Dad—cried a lot and thought that everything was just totally unfair." Claudia paused and walked toward the window. She stared for a long while at the bright orange moon set in an otherwise black sky.

"I guess I'm telling you this because I learnt a lot from what's supposed to be a bad thing. We kids and Mom grew

closer than before and we all used resources we never
would've developed in a 'happy' home. We really relied on
each other and I realized how good people can be, if you
give them half a chance. Looking intent, Claudia nodded
her head. "It was a rough period but, you know, now that I
look back on it, I'm glad that it happened."

Abruptly stopping, Claudia laughed and looked at me.
"Hey, you've really got me talking about myself!"

I smiled. I felt relaxed, almost contented. "I don't
mind," I assured her. "A lot of what you've said makes me
think back to Bristol."

Pushing away her dinner plate and resting her chin on
her palm, Claudia smiled encouragingly. "Like what? I'd
really like to know."

I reflected for a moment. "My family always pushed
academic achievement and, okay, I guess that was good.
But emotionally they really held back." I mentioned that in
high school and college I had pursued good grades more
than anything else and joked that during my freshman
year in college I had believed that straight A's would be-
stow instant acceptance by beautiful women as well as
eternal happiness.

"Damn, those were wasted years." I shook my head as if
to purge myself of the memory. "But in Bristol I looked
back, back at what I'd really enjoyed in life and what I'd
emphasize if given another chance.

"Claud, I suddenly realized that academic stuff like,
well, making Dean's list or being a Harvard Ph.D. means
diddlyshit. What I really liked are people—Peace Corps
work or my friendships."

I reached for my wine but discovered that I had no taste
for it. Turning back to Claudia I mentioned, "It must be ter-
rible to be seventy years old and dying and only then re-ex-
amine your life seriously for the first time. To see similar
mistakes stretching over fifty years must be frustrating.
But what's even worse is that when you're seventy you
can't do anything about it."

Claudia nodded agreement and asked what I saw myself doing now.

"The thesis. Then I'm free from school. This year I'm going to finish the thesis even if it kills me. Further down the road I want to start a family. Until the operation I enjoyed jumping from relationship to relationship. Now, I don't."

I looked past Claudia to her glowering ancestor and thought back to my grandfather's house in Bristol and how, as a ten-year-old kid, I had spent rainy afternoons wandering among oil portraits of various Howes and trying to guess who had been kind, amusing, or cruel. Even as a child I had enjoyed being one of the more recent members in a family that could trace itself back some four hundred years.

"I don't know why we have families," I suggested to Claudia. "Perhaps by leaving part of us after we die we can believe that our lives have been of value."

"And you're not afraid to admit that you want to get married and have children?"

"No," I replied. "It's a natural feeling."

"You sure enjoy your nieces and nephews," she noted. "Especially the youngest one, the cute kid who plays classical violin and strangles cats." Claudia smiled and looked thoughtfully at me for a long time. "I'm getting to know more about you and I like it," she finally said. "It's sad that we had to wait until tonight."

She hesitated as she poured the remains of the wine into my glass. "In one of my oriental courses at Berkeley I remember reading that the Chinese ideograph for crisis has two symbols. One means danger. The other stands for opportunity." Tilting her wine glass, Claudia watched the red Burgundy slosh from side to side, approaching yet never flowing over the glass's lip. Finally she said, "Maybe this cancer'll be a blessing in disguise, just like Mother's leaving Dad."

We walked into the dimly lit living room; three hours of

sitting on kitchen chairs had been enough. Claudia
hunched herself over the piano and intently banged out a
few discordant bars of "The Star Spangled Banner." She
looked up when I started to laugh. "It's the only song I
know," she defiantly announced, "and I taught myself how
to play it in the third grade." But then she grinned and
stretched her arms in mock outrage. "But even then my
music teacher said that I was totally tone deaf. I didn't care
too much, though. God, I was so small that my feet
couldn't reach the pedals and I always worried that people
would see my legs and those mousy-looking white socks
dangling in midair."

We strolled onto the porch. The wind was blowing
slightly as large pine branches scratched against the
screen windows. Claudia rested her head on my arm and
looked absently at the pine trees. "I don't know, Herb," she
said slowly. "I get angry at you, sometimes joke a lot, but
now I know that I really like you. I'm hoping that you get
through the cancer and, who knows, maybe even gain from
it." Claudia thought for a moment and looked up at me.
"When you were talking about getting out of school, find-
ing a job you really want, and raising a family, I kept
imagining that Picasso print. You know, the one where two
hands are grasping some colored flowers? Well, okay, I
know that it's corny and all that, but whenever I look at it I
think that we're here on earth for just a short while so, hey,
why not grab life and squeeze it for all it's worth?" Claudia
shrugged self-deprecatingly. "It's so easy to say that, of
course, and I sure get angry at myself for not doing more
than I do.

"But Herb," she continued, "the big question is
whether you'll take advantage of what other people con-
sider to be tragedy or, with your past glibness, will you pass
it off as 'just another event?' Until tonight I thought you
couldn't change. Show me I was wrong."

I looked at my right wrist. Over the last few days both
the pain and edema had lessened. My second finger, which

couldn't move after the operation, could now cautiously inch up and down.

Claudia swirled the wine around in her glass. "When you were in Bristol and assuming that you might die, you thought of things which you wished you had done. Do them now. If there's a god, he's given you a second chance. The more you do, the more you'll discover about yourself. And Herb," Claudia paused, "I really want you to do it."

At midnight I said that I must leave. Standing in the foyer I looked down at Claudia. The moonlight shone upon her face. We were leaving and probably would not see each other again. Yet, I felt quietly exuberant.

Various relatives and friends had generously contributed their time and concern after the operation. Unlike most, Claudia had been direct and often critical. Her feisty attitude indicated that she still regarded me an equal, as somebody who didn't need condolences or money. Claudia had given me one of the most precious gifts a patient may have: dignity.

At Claudia's urging I had laid open my feelings. Having to respond to her questions and criticisms, I was forced to look at some of the fears which other friends had hesitated to discuss. Having to deal with the fears, I felt relief; they now appeared beatable. "If I still have cancer," I thought, "I'll now be able to fight back."

Most of all, I now regarded any existing cancer as a challenge, an opponent, an important game. I thought of Claudia and her father. Could cancer push me beyond what I thought had been my limits?

Holding hands we stood together for several minutes and gazed at the enlarged shadows of tree branches swaying across the floor. I turned and walked with Claudia onto the front steps. The early September air had turned crisp at night, yet the street lamps, picking up the slowly oranging and yellowing leaves, lent a warmth to the evening.

I looked at Claudia and smiled appreciatively. "You're a

tremendous person. I enjoyed what you said tonight. It doesn't matter whether we see each other again. It's been a tremendous experience knowing you. I'll never forget you. You're just fine."

Claudia grinned and hugged me. "And so are you, Herb. And so are you."

Nodding her head she said "I think we'll see each other again. People who care for each other somehow find a means of getting together."

A wave of sadness flowed through me. Then I looked at Claudia for the last time. She simply nodded and we kissed goodby. I turned and walked back to my jeep.

Driving over the Lars Anderson bridge I glanced at the looming silhouettes of the Prudential and Hancock buildings and the moonlight upon the Charles River. The brief sadness had departed; Claudia had infected me with a sense of purpose.

It was one-thirty in the morning and I felt exhilarated. "Screw sleep," I decided as I strolled through Harvard Yard, past a still brightly lit Square and then across the quadrangle outside Langdell law library. Across the street, a cluster of high school townies were perching on two of their muscle cars, swilling beer, and recalling past victories.

Down one and then the other side of the Quad. I thought of past accomplishments and failures and of how, if I had worked harder, I could have done far better.

An hour later I was walking by the dark brick Pound Building, around the statue of the crouching discus thrower at Hemenway Gym, and then back to Langdell Quadrangle.

"Claudia's right," I concluded. "Do what you want to do and do it well. This year I'll finish that thesis. She doesn't think I can change. But change can't stop at some arbitrary age. I'll show her. And, of course, I've got to try new things, be more open to different people."

I kicked at some oak leaves and thought of how all of us are in a race against time. "We can't win but maybe we'll gain honorable mention if we do as much as we possibly can. Satisfaction, not winning. That's the best we should expect."

At four o'clock I climbed the steps of my summer apartment for the last time. Soon I would be living in Harvard Square. I lay on my bed and thought of old goals which were now worthless to me and wondered how best to accomplish the new ones. As the sun rose I smiled and gave silent thanks for Claudia. A few hours later I was flying home to see my parents in Madison.

# Three

THE NEXT FEW WEEKS proved uneventful. While in Madison, my parents expressed relief that my doctors had removed the tumor. My father, who audits courses at the medical school as well as teaching "Greek and Latin Medical Terms," expressed special delight in reading my medical report. But we didn't discuss cancer very often; after all, I was healthy. Emily, my younger sister and a former student in Greece, treated my parents and me to a sumptuous Greek feast the night before I left for Massachusetts. I had enjoyed the vacation, but spurred on by my Maine professorship and my last night with Claudia I was impatient to begin my final school year. As the airline limousine arrived the next day my father grabbed a suitcase and walked with me down the driveway. "Don't forget that we're here. And, uh, if the cancer does come back, let us know what we can do." I grinned and blithefully repeated the Tumor Board's prognosis of clear health.

"The evening had gone really well. I thought the time was right so I bent down to kiss her." It was a late November evening and Jack, a former student of mine, was striving to entertain me with his recent sexual peccadilloes.

"But, suddenly she pushed away from me, covered her chest, and blurted something about saving herself for marriage." Jack grimaced. "That's the last time I'll ever have a blind date with a Mt. Ida student."

Something else was on my mind; I could not concentrate on Jack. When he excused himself to go to the bathroom, I picked up the phone and began dialing.

A drowsy woman's voice answered.

"Donna, it's Herb and I'm sorry to bother you but I'd like to speak with Bill."

A series of whispers, a resigned grunt, and Bill picked up the phone.

"Bill? Herb. Look, I'm having chemotherapy and I'll really need some dope of yours. Do you have any left?"

"Yeah but, hey, I thought that your doctors had ruled out chemotherapy, that you didn't need it."

I bit my lower lip. Telling friends about the doctors' new decision would be difficult.

"Last Monday my radiologists and then my oncologist told me that a review of my biopsy shows a very high chance of the cancer still being inside me and growing rapidly. Already it may have spread to other parts of the body. Chemotherapy is essential but difficult. My oncologist says that marijuana will help me get through it."

"Oh, shit." Bill was silent for a moment. "Then it's really bad, isn't it?"

The first two months of school had proved busy. As a resident tutor I initiated a speakers series that brought numerous government and academic leaders to Dudley House. Also at Harvard I was aiding Professor Martin Kilson teach two courses in African politics while teaching a similar course myself.

Each Wednesday afternoon I boarded a Greyhound bus in Boston to teach "Politics of Developing Nations" at the University of Maine. I would arrive in Portland in the early evening, play squash with a fellow faculty member, teach my course, and sprint the mile back to the bus station for the final Boston bus. By one o'clock I was back in Boston.

The combination of cancer forcing me to re-evaluate

my life and Claudia's reflections during our last night together had thoroughly convinced me that I should rapidly complete my thesis and, more important, that I should live every day as if it was my last. I had already written one hundred and forty pages of my thesis and planned to graduate in June. Since I spent two hours each day travelling to Peter Bent Brigham hospital for radiation treatments, I was looking forward to completing the treatments and finishing my thesis.

On a Tuesday in mid-October I was outside the radiation clinic and bending over a cantankerous water fountain when I felt a tug on my jeans. A small girl with blonde hair and incredibly large blue eyes smiled up at me. She was clutching a Raggedy Ann doll.

"My name's Gloria and I'm six years old," she announced.

"I'm Herb," I replied. "And I'm thirty-one years old."

Gloria's eyes widened further. "Wow, that's old!" And as I slowly shook my head, she scampered into the waiting room.

The X-ray waiting room at Brigham had been thoughtfully decorated with several plants, table lamps, and innumerable magazines donated by the staff or former patients. But after perfunctorily thumbing through the nearest publication, most of us would gaze vacantly into the center of the room.

Despite seeing each other five days a week, we rarely conversed. All of us knew that fifty percent would die within the next twelve months. Understandably, we were hesitant to intrude on someone's privacy or to form new friendships. A quiet camaraderie did exist. We would smile as each patient came in, offer chairs to infirm patients, or pick up knitting needles dropped by some of the elderly women. But we invariably performed such politenesses with a minimum of conversation.

Whatever talk did occur would center upon our particular maladies. Most of us picked up and, often with delight, would trip off our tongues the Latin names of our illnesses:

adenocarcinoma, osteogenesis, histiocytic fibrosarcoma, as well as other passwords—mitosis, remission, rads, photon, cobalt, and protocol.

An intruding outsider might have labeled us as conceited and indeed a year or so earlier each of us would have disdained this mystical medical gobbledygook. Perhaps we now felt we could better deal with our cancers by demystifying them. Rather than retreat by referring to "our illnesses," the appropriate terminology would single out and thus limit our cancer. Such polysyllabic esoterica conferred more status than words like illness, cancer, or for that matter mumps, measles, gout, or cramps. Finally, we undoubtedly enjoyed the temporary fantasy of pretending to be doctors. In my case, my knowledge generally ended with impressive labels. Fortunately, most people feared to inquire any further.

Yet, however quietly, all of us suffered with Gloria. Her youth and attractiveness epitomized the tragedy of indiscriminate cancer. Within the last three years, Gloria had undergone three operations and two years of radiation. Every morning she and her mother would enter, check in at the reception desk, and take a seat. Gloria invariably clutched her doll. By bouncing it upon her knee, she escorted her doll to familiar places: the supermarket, school, or a friend's house. Never to the hospital.

After five or ten minutes of playing with the doll, Gloria would look intensely at her mother. Still clutching Raggedy Ann, Gloria would sit straight up in the chair. Her eyes would dart quickly from the hallway, to Raggedy Ann, and then back to the hallway. Each of us watched Gloria, felt compassion for her and yet rarely, if ever, did we try to comfort her with words.

Eventually Rochelle or Susie, the two radiation attendants, would enter the waiting room and smile at Gloria. "It really breaks us up inside," Susie later told me, "to bring Gloria in. She's an incredible kid, just coming here each morning and waiting for us."

When Gloria saw them, understanding and fear filled

her wide eyes. Tears trickled down and she grabbed her mother. She kicked and screamed as Rochelle, Susie, and her mother strove to comfort her. Finally, with incredible bravery, Gloria slowly let go of her mother. Still clutching Raggedy Ann, she slowly walked to the young attendant. Together they walked down the hall.

A few minutes later, as a child's screams of anguish shot down the hall, we looked at the potted plants or turned to a magazine.

"What will happen to Gloria?" I once asked Rochelle.

"We assume she'll die. Probably within a year."

"Why not let her live normally?" I asked. "It might be shorter than if she had radiation but it would sure be more pleasant."

Rochelle sighed and lifted her hands in a gesture of total helplessness. "We have to hope that we're wrong, that Gloria's an exception. Or, that somewhere in some lab a researcher is developing an experimental antidote to her form of adenocarcinoma. I guess with every cancer patient we really are in a race with time. Consider the money and the brains we've got working with us. We hope that no patient'll ever give up on us."

Despite the general lack of conversation, I became friendly with a woman whose last name I never learnt. She was a large, florid individual with wispy gray hair, whom, because she closely resembled Margaret Rutherford in several Agatha Christie films, I called "Miss Marple." Both Miss Marple and her husband, Arthur, had developed cancer within a year of each other.

For forty years they had lived and worked in Scituate, one of Boston's bedroom communities. When her husband became stricken with cancer, Miss Marple was in shock for several months. "I had always heard about cancer" she said, "but I never worried about it. I thought it was a disease that only other people got."

Miss Marple came out of shock to help her increasingly inactive husband by learning basic carpentry and auto repair and by driving to hospitals and to a declining number of social events. "Both of us wanted to be with each other during the time we had left rather than spend it with other people."

Miss Marple continued by explaining that cancer brought them closer together. "For example, we didn't argue about the usual petty things. Now that both of us have it, we understand what the other is going through. We spend most of each day helping each other. Of course I'm a lot healthier than he is, so I'm happy doing most of the work."

I looked at Arthur. He was shorter and skinnier than his stolid wife. Arthur invariably wore a dark business suit with an equally dark overcoat. On his suit lapel was a small red flower. Behind his large glasses were small furtive eyes which would wander about the waiting room, never stopping long enough to indicate a special interest in anything.

When a radiation nurse or secretary would ask him something, he would smile wanly and Miss Marple would quickly answer for him. After both of them had finished their daily treatments, Miss Marple would quietly take her husband's hand, assist him up, and keep him on her arm as they shuffled down the yellow corridor.

For my first two weeks I had said nothing to Miss Marple. Occasionally when I looked about the room, I was greeted by an inquisitive yet warm smile from her. Then one morning I limped into the quiet waiting room. My right knee was throbbing with pain from running the day before. As I eased myself into a chair I heard a soft, clear voice ask, "Young man, are you much of an athlete?"

I turned to face Miss Marple. "Well, I don't know," I stammered. "I try to be, but my body always gives out on me."

She nodded sagely. "Don't overdo it," she offered, "but never stop your physical activity. And, what is it you do?"

"Most anything recently," I replied. "Football, running, swimming, squash."

"Good heavens." Her eyebrows shot upwards and she smiled at me. "I wish I had done all those things when I was your age. Time just rushes by."

We started talking about how we had reacted to hearing that we had cancer. "Sometimes we people are so daffy," Miss Marple said as she studied me. "We jabber incessantly about things that'll mean absolutely crumbs tomorrow. But we ignore crucial things, like our health."

"Perhaps that's necessary," I uncertainly offered.

"Rubbish," she rejoined. "If we even took a bit more time to look at life seriously—the fact that we're going to die perhaps sooner than we think—then we'd work harder with the time we have left. And, if we do live a long life, then we'll have enjoyed it so much the more."

I looked at the four other patients. Gloria was silently moving Raggedy's legs to an unknown destination. Two patients were quietly listening to Miss Marple. Her husband sat unmoving in his chair. When I looked closely, his eyes somehow seemed more animated, warmer than before.

Miss Marple hesitated and then lowered her voice. "May I ask about your condition?"

I nodded and briefly told her about the early scare followed by the prediction of an excellent recovery. Miss Marple smiled. "That's nice, so very nice," she offered. "You've been face to face with cancer and you've survived. Young man, may I suggest this? Take your knowledge and your health and run with them through life. Fighters stand a better chance."

Friday, November 19th, bestowed upon Boston a charmingly crisp and sunny fall day. I woke early and ambled up Holyoke Street towards Dudley House.

In the early morning the streets winding around Harvard Square's kiosk are relatively quiet and the air smells fresh and clean. The chubby and rubicund Irishmen wearing their cloth caps are snipping the strings from the *Bos-*

*ton Globe* and *The New York Times*. To their friends they impart sage observations ranging from the state of the Red Sox to the glories of the late arrant mayor, James Curley. Across the street from the island kiosk, employees from Brigham's restaurant and the Harvard Coop chat leisurely before they begin another day's work.

I purchased a *Globe* and *Times* at the kiosk. I bid "Good Morning" to a stooped old gentleman who for years has wandered around Cambridge with a sandwich sign proclaiming "Abortion Is Murder." I crossed Mass Ave to Dudley House where I enjoyed a whopping six-pancake breakfast. The day promised no distractions, no problems.

Aboard the yellow Harvard shuttle bus I watched the bleary-eyed medical students mount the steps and slump resignedly into the seats. They soon commenced an unconscious ritual. Breaking the silence, one student would speculate about a recent assignment and donate his analysis. As the bus bounced along the M.I.T. bridge, wound its way through Back Bay and then skirted the pastoral Fenway, other students joined the discussion. When the bus pulled to its final stop at the intersection of Louis Pasteur Avenue and Longwood Avenue, the future doctors would be ready for another grueling day of study.

Inside the radiation ward's waiting room I noticed that neither Gloria nor Miss Marple was present. Fortunately, the wait was short. Within ten minutes I was lying on my back with my wrist encased in a plaster cast. As usual, a technician smiled, said "This won't hurt a bit," and then retreated behind a thick lead shield.

Overhead, the four million volt linear accelerator hummed its way towards me, clicking upon arriving, and then reverted to a deeper hum which indicated that two hundred rads were shooting into my wrist, stopping, and then modifying whatever living cells remained within the specified area of six by thirteen centimeters. After several weeks, the skin on my right wrist had become fibrosed and hard.

Radiation therapy is an often painless and effective agent against cancer. It eradicates some cancers while controlling the growth and lessening the pain of others.

Radiation does not kill cells; rather, it damages their reproductive capacity. Cancer cells divide more rapidly than normal cells and therefore are more susceptible to radiation. When a cancer cell hit by radiation reaches the end of its lifespan, it dies without reproducing.

I climbed down from the platform and buttoned my right sleeve. The radiation attendants were young and bright and very solicitous. We joked about this being one of my last trips and how I could use my radioactive wrist as a nightlight.

Dr. Greenwalter escorted me to the waiting room. As usual, he bantered about his banjo and trumpet playing, conjecturing that the musical world desperately needed a fresh personality. As we neared the waiting room, Greenwalter touched me on the elbow and motioned towards a small cul-de-sac. His voice quickly changed tone.

"Your treatments are concluding, Herb, and unless Dr. Grey does definitely prescribe chemotherapy, you'll have more time for your thesis." I nodded and thanked him for his and Dr. Ott's assistance.

Chemotherapy. On the bus back to Harvard I jerked upright. The day had lost its soothing casualness and gained a frightening intensity. Two months earlier Grey had loftily dismissed chemotherapy: "I really don't picture it for you. It would be a last resort." Now Greenwalter was mentioning chemotherapy as a possibility.

Had the pathologists discovered a tumor? Did I still have cancer? Was it unstoppable? What would happen to my thesis? Was I going to live or die?

When I arrived home, I called the radiation ward. Both Greenwalter and Ott were out. I received the same response from Dr. Grey's secretary. My mind flashed back to late July and those four days of waiting. I was discovering that people who have had cancer live with an on-going, daily uncertainty. Do they still have cancer? Will it return?

Over Saturday's breakfast I decided not to call Ott or Grey until Monday. I knew that if I could not reach them, which was likely, that fear would build upon fear. Every unanswered phonecall would swell a growing anxiety. I wished to prove that I could control my feelings by transferring my tension elsewhere.

That afternoon I circled, stalked, and pummelled the gym's heavy bag for an hour. I sought and gratefully received a vote of confidence from the large wall mirrors. Rivulets of sweat sparkled as they trickled down my still tan body. My red face bore a happy, frenzied look. "Hell," I informed the mirror, "I ain't got no cancer." Slipping off my gloves and handwraps, I plunged into the brisk fall day and ran five miles along the Charles River. Then I sprinted up the steps of the Indoor Athletic Building and swam until closing time.

That night I had dinner with Jane at the Old Oyster House. Cloistered in a dark corner with a flickering yellow candle playing upon a checkered tablecloth, I felt completely relaxed. Ever since she had introduced me to Claudia, I had liked Jane and now I deeply appreciated her concern for my health. I mentioned Greenwalter's hint of chemotherapy but brushed it off as probably insignificant, ignoring Jane's obviously concerned scrutiny.

"But Herb," Jane insisted. "Did he say anything else about chemo, about your condition?" She flicked at her hair. "I can't believe that he would have said something that would worry you unless he had a reason."

We looked at each other for a long time. Jane's long blonde hair had cascaded onto her gray angora sweater. As usual, her aqua-green eyes evinced sympathy and understanding. I appreciated her presence.

Finally I responded. "I'm in the quandary of having to worry about my health yet not allowing my fears to bother me. Repression is a good thing," I thought aloud, "if the alternative is moping about and thinking the worst. Maybe that's why I've been doing more sports."

Jane squeezed my hand and smiled her understanding.

She had helped her best friend and her younger sister through chemotherapy. "Let's not worry about it now," she said softly, "but whatever comes up, I'll be there."

On Monday I arrived half an hour early for treatment. Again, neither the young girl nor Miss Marple was there. When Dr. Ott ushered me into the radiation room I asked him about chemotherapy.

"Why do you ask?"

"Because Dr. Greenwalter mentioned it last Friday and I don't believe that you casually drop such scare words to your patients."

"Come over here, Herb." Ott motioned to the same cul-de-sac off the main hallway. I felt eerily calm, almost knowing what he would say.

"First of all, you're to see Dr. Grey as soon as possible." He paused and considered his next words.

"Three months ago, when Dr. Dunn excised your tumor, the biopsies indicated a slow growth tumor. We rank tumors on a one to three basis. One is no or slow growth and relatively safe. Three is fast growing and cause for concern. Do you know what mitosis is?"

"Cell division," I responded. High school biology had finally paid a dividend.

"Right." Ott adjusted his glasses. "Well, we've re-examined your biopsies and we now believe that you definitely have a number three situation. The cancer cells display an alarmingly aggressive mitosis. Frankly, we're very concerned. Dr. Grey has recommended that you consult with him about receiving chemotherapy."

Fear was grabbing me. Never before had doctors encountered any problems diagnosing my ailments. Yet broken bones and the mumps lay well within the purview of medical skills. Now I felt that I had crossed a threshold separating ignorance and irrationality from the enlightenment and the rationality that I had expected from all medical experts. I speculated that any medical rescue attempts could only be well-meaning forays into unexplored areas.

I also felt anger. Why had they kept the biopsy news from me for seven weeks? I could not believe that only now had they decided to re-evaluate my biopsy slides. I bitterly concluded that the doctors had decided that I could not take all the news in one blow. By that evening much of my bitterness had subsided. Rather than cursing the bad news, I was criticizing its messengers. Blaming experts who were working hard for my survival seemed a misplacement of frustration. Instead, Grey and I had to work together to nullify any remaining cancer.

Inside Dr. Grey's office, efficient secretaries and pictures of rugged outdoor settings contrasted with quiet and inordinately intense cancer patients waiting to talk with their oncologists. I sank into a deep chair and reviewed the questions I would ask Grey.

Thomas Grey is a large muscular man who must remind people of a middle-aged Jack Dempsey. His soft deliberate speech belies an enormous intensity of feeling and power which reassures many distraught patients.

"We've recently looked again at your biopsies," Grey began as he skimmed through my file. "At first Dunn's excellent excision seemed good enough. But, due to the great rarity of your cancer, we decided to put you through photon and neutron radiation. Now, the biopsies strongly suggest that we begin chemotherapy."

He abruptly stopped. Although he was still hunched over my file, I sensed that he was waiting for questions.

, "Is it necessary?"

"Absolutely."

"How long will chemotherapy last?"

"Presently we're contemplating a six months' protocol."

I inwardly groaned. Chemotherapy threatened my June graduation. "Can I begin the treatments in March or April?"

"No. I want you to begin as soon as possible. We have a protocol already set up and its effectiveness would be seriously damaged if we wait until spring."

Dr. Grey has achieved a high reputation as an oncologist, whereas I knew very little about cancer, chemotherapy, or the importance of my biopsies. Reluctantly I consented to begin chemotherapy.

Grey nodded appreciatively. "I'd like you to call my office this Wednesday. We'll have established the time and place for your first treatment."

Tilting back in his swivel chair he studied me. "Now, as you probably know, until recently we didn't administer chemotherapy unless it was absolutely necessary." Grey looked up at me. "Herb, you fit that category. Now, chemo is often the best treatment but it does induce several very unpleasant side effects."

So chemotherapy was "absolutely necessary" for me. I sat stunned as Grey reeled off what would happen to me: severe nausea and prolonged vomiting accompanied by diarrhea, lethargy, and possible anemia. "If chemo is a medicine, then who needs a disease?" I wondered.

Grey concluded his lexicon of terrors by leaning forward and folding his hands. "And, of course, you will lose your hair—all, or practically all, of it. It's nothing really to worry about. Almost all the patients obtain wigs and appear remarkably attractive."

"Permanent baldness?" I stammered.

"Not at all. Your hair does grow back and the only changes might be a slight curliness and a slightly darker color to it." He softly smiled. "Off the record, the change does some of the patients good."

I sat still, wondering what other surprises would spring forth. Grey cleared his throat and thought for a few seconds, "I should emphasize that chemotherapy is not a foolproof cure. With your protocol, approximately fifty percent of the patients gained significant tumor regression." What, I silently wondered, had happened to the remaining fifty percent?

"I know this is an unfair question, Doctor, but what are my chances of living?"

"Pretty good, I hope. Yours is an interesting case because of its rarity and because this is the first time we'll be using this particular protocol on a histiocytic fibrosarcoma."

He quickly continued. "The three drugs are of the C.A.D. protocol: Cytoxan, Adriamycin, and DTIC." He carefully wrote their names on an index card which he pushed across his desk to me. The terms meant nothing to me then. During the following months I would not be able to repeat the three names without my stomach tightening and my mouth having a slight taste of nausea.

"We'll give you two of these three drugs for two consecutive days every three weeks. It's what we call combination therapy. We've discovered that two or more drugs administered together or right after each other have a better effect than if given separately."

Thesis considerations still plagued my conscience. "Is there anything I can do to lessen the therapy's adverse effects?"

Grey considered my question and then wryly smiled. "Well, yes, but if you understand that I'm not talking to you in an official capacity as your doctor . . ." His voice trailed off and he searched my face for comprehension. I nodded and he continued.

"To counteract some of the pain and vomiting we used to give THC—marijuana—to our patients. For largely political reasons we've stopped this practice. But marijuana is a good thing. I'd recommend that you obtain some of it." As I later learned, the chemotherapy affects the chemoreceptor trigger zone (CTZ) in the brain. The CTZ's nerve fibers stimulate the brain's vomit center, whose own nerve fibers cause the diaphragm and stomach muscles to contract. Marijuana, more than Compazine or other antiemetics, prevent the drugs from affecting the CTZ.

As Grey walked me to the door he cautioned, "It'll be no picnic. Each time you'll feel worse. Expect it and take it in stride." I thanked him and assured him that for medici-

nal purposes I would obtain some marijuana. So on a blus-
tery Monday afternoon I completed a lecture on Rhodesian
politics and met Bill at the foot of Widener Library. He
elaborately bowed and presented me with two long, tapered
joints.

"Après moi, le déluge?" Bill laughingly inquired.

"Don't ever base your life on forecasts," I replied as we
repaired to the Faculty Club for drinks. "Procrastination
never accomplishes anything."

Would my hair really fall out? Could I handle the
chemo? What would happen to my thesis? During the next
day I went through the usual motion of work but kept
speculating on the upcoming chemo.

On Tuesday evening I spent three quiet hours in front
of my fireplace. I needed consolation, warmth, and the re-
assurance of a successful past before my first session. As
the hissing wood cast forth undulating waves of flame, I
reached back into my memory for people and events. I
thought of Claudia on the first date, dressed in a print dress
of tiny flowers, deeply tanned, and smiling inquisitively at
me with those large olive black eyes. I hoped to see her
again; our last night together had given me a new spirit. As
Jane had said on Saturday night, "Claudia really opened a
door in your mind and let a lot of fresh air blow in."

The phone rang. Jon and Norah asked if I needed any
help tomorrow. I reassured them that I could handle every-
thing.

"How can you tell?" Jon countered.

"Well, at least I need to try everything by myself," I
replied. "Then if I do need help, I'll know that I gave it my
best effort."

We said goodby and my mind drifted back ten years to
two events of my Peace Corps service in midwest Nigeria. I
was a twenty-year-old college teacher in a village of several
thousand residents, no electricity, and little running water.
One day I was explaining a difficult passage in Words-
worth's poem "Michael" when a student with a perplexed

frown suddenly sat straight up. His eyes widened and when he caught my quizzical look, he smiled broadly and nodded. I had broken through; I had helped him understand.

Two of my closest friends were Ibos named Molokwu and Enwokeji. I had opened up to them and they more than amply responded. During my year and a half we played tennis, debated Nigerian politics, joked about the white Irish missionaries, and chased after the same women. When the Biafran army suddenly invaded our small town Molokwu and Enwokeji and his wife interrupted their frantic packing to spend a hasty last lunch with me. Since their lives were in danger, I was both amazed and pleased that they would spare the time to say goodby. Against Enwokeji's whispered protestations, I quietly thrust a ten pound note into his hand. Then I watched them drive out to an uncertain future. They had been the first black people whose skin color proved irrelevant to me. They were friends whom I could count on when needed. I never saw them again.

And then the night in Massachusetts with Sarah, the first night I had told a woman that I loved her and truly believed it. We lay next to each other at three in the morning gazing rapturously into each others' eyes, untalking.

Thinking over these incidents I realized that by giving of myself emotionally to another person I had received more than I had ever expected. By eleven o'clock I felt at peace with myself and rested, ready for whatever might happen the following day. I lifted the receiver off the hook and quickly fell asleep.

On Wednesday morning I crossed the street to Stillman Infirmary for a blood test. I asked the medical technician about the test's significance.

She smiled. "Everyone I test at Harvard asks me incredible questions about the results. I'll be happy to explain the test to you, but only once.

"You'll be having a CBC—a complete blood count. The

major considerations are your platelet and white blood count. The plats serve as your clotting mechanism. Chemotherapy decreases their number. It's possible, although unlikely, that if you fall out of bed in two months' time you could hemorrhage internally—the brain, for example." She stopped and looked challengingly at me. "Do you want me to continue?"

"Sure." I replied. "What have I got to lose?"

"Okay, the white blood count will serve as the most important single test. A normal person has a WBC between 6,000 and 9,000 whites per field measure. Chemotherapy damages the bone marrow, which produces the whites. Since the whites prevent infection, you're vastly more susceptible to diseases during chemo. Serious problems arise when a patient has to receive regular dosages but his white count is so low that he's picking up various infections. If your white count slips below 2,700, Dr. Grey will probably delay your chemo treatment."

Walking back through the waiting room I observed a now familiar scene in the corner: a young, dark-haired man cradling a gaunt, near scarecrow of a woman. Three years earlier when he had taught me international economics, the students had judged Professor Williams to be an unfeeling martinet. Williams based the final grade upon 4,500 pages of reading and a term paper. He brooked no excuses or suggestions about lessening the reading. "You're here in school to learn. You learn by reading and writing." Apparently determined to rise rapidly within the academic hierarchy, Williams refused to meet with students outside of class. He spent most of his day in his office, writing books and magazine articles.

To us he epitomized the lack of concern for students that is such an integral part of graduate school. Now I saw him futilely trying to hold back tears as his atrophying wife nestled against him. Williams glanced up. I had hesitated too long in my walk. He nodded in apparent recognition and then looked away. I walked on, embarrassed that I had intruded upon a personal moment.

Crossing over the trolley tracks on Commonwealth Avenue, I reflected upon the demands that cancer must place upon a marriage. When they had married seven years ago, the Williamses seemed to have everything: fine educations, mutual academic and athletic interests, sufficient incomes, and a promising future. Since graduating from Smith in the mid-1960's, Paula Williams had written a book, won several tennis tournaments, and had been one of the most attractive faculty wives. Now she was a terminal cancer patient and weighed sixty-three pounds. A few straggly hairs lay atop an otherwise bald head. A close family friend had told me that she spent much of each day doubled over in pain from the combined radiation-chemotherapy treatments and worrying that her illness was forcing her husband into a debt that he would be paying long after she died.

"In sickness or in health" now bore a new meaning for me. Mrs. Williams was a different woman from a year before and surely the illness must have sparked tension between them. Yet my supposedly hard-bitten professor would leave his study in Harvard Yard every morning to chauffeur his wife to the Deaconess, comfort her while they waited for an available machine, and then drive her back to Lexington. Was I seeing a different side of my former professor, I wondered, or had cancer tapped a reservoir of unused emotion and caring?

A few hours later I was strolling through a leaf-covered Harvard Yard, self-consciously drawing in on Bill's marijuana while ignoring the giggles and heads turning around. At the bus, I pinched the half-finished joint and waited until I stepped off the bus before relighting it. Languorously strolling up Longwood Avenue, I imagined this scene with a policeman.

"All right, buddy. Let's have that grass and some identification. This stuff ain't legal, ya know."

"But officer," I would reply. "I've got a fatal cancer and doctors have advised me to smoke this before I take intravenous chemotherapy." The erstwhile belligerent cop in my fantasy would stammer an effusive apology, vigorously pat me on the back, and allow me to proceed.

No policeman appeared. I giddily floated into the Outpatient Building at Deaconess Hospital. An old rock tune, "Rocking Robin" captured my mind and body. I bounced up to an information desk and, grinning broadly, asked for the chemotherapy ward. The attendant gave me a puzzled look and pointed to her left.

A chemotherapy ward is no laughing matter. Almost everyone is old and cognizant that they may have only a few days left of life. Some of the patients are hunched over resignedly in wheelchairs waiting for the toxic transfusions which may give a few months or possibly years. Emaciated, wide-eyed, and seemingly uncomprehending, they reminded me of Margaret Bourke-White's photographs of recently liberated concentration camp inmates. You can sense a tenseness within the ward, a tenseness which is betrayed only by a patient's quiet sobbing or by the insistent tapping of fingers against a wheelchair.

Into this somber setting I bounced, blissfully snapping my fingers and humming, "Rockin' Robin" ("Rock in the treetop all night long, Rockin' robin, rock, rock, rock . . .").

A thoughtful secretary had baked a large plateful of brownies. I asked a now bemused nurse if the brownies were for the patients. Without answering she asked, "Are you Mr. Howe and have you been smoking marijuana?"

I smiled conspiratorially, jiggled my eyebrows and replied, "Guilty on both accounts." She relented. "You've got the munchies and the brownies haven't been touched all day. Go ahead and finish them."

I attacked the brownies and was scooping up the few remaining crumbs when the chemotherapist emerged from a rear room and inquired, "Is a Mr. Howe here?"

Reclining in a padded plastic chair resembling those found in dentists' offices, I examined my latest doctor with interest. Her long, attractive body and blonde hair hinted at long off-hours spent on the tennis court. She handed me an

Informed Consent statement on which I only vaguely noted the list of bad side effects and that "Your physicians have considered your individual situation and have concluded that at this time, no other therapeutic approaches such as surgery, radiotherapy, or other chemotherapeutic treatments are clinically indicated as being effective."

As I rolled up my left sleeve, the chemotherapist coaxed an intravenous "tree," or stand into position. She deftly hooked a 150 cubic centimeter container of saline solution to the top and ran the tubing down to my arm. To the tubing she attached a small butterfly needle and, with a quick wink at me, jabbed the needle into my wrist.

"We'll be ready in a second," she estimated. "I guess with all that marijuana you're feeling just fine."

But, at that moment she placed in front of me what appeared to be inhumanly long needles and syringes containing orange and white liquids. While marijuana frequently produces exhilaration it may also trigger acute paranoia which renders its user a hapless wretch.

I stared at her display. Clutching the chair's arms and leaning forward I hollowly inquired, "Is that all for me?"

"Yes, and it really won't hurt very much," she primly responded as she gently pushed me back into the chair.

The blonde chemotherapist sat next to me after inserting the Adriamycin syringe and needle into the IV tubing. Holding my wrist just below the needle, she strove to keep my panicking mind off the colored liquid slowly snaking its way down the clear tube.

Chemotherapy is a fairly new method of treating cancer. The major advantage of drugs is their ability to reach areas impervious to a surgeon's knife or a machine's ray. Because of its various side effects it is usually prescribed for patients who have had both surgery and radiation and still face at least a moderate possibility of dying.

Once the drugs enter the bloodstream they spread throughout the body. The chemicals affect only rapidly dividing cells. Cancer cells are often rapidly dividing. Unfortunately, so are the healthy cells in the bone marrow, hair follicles, and the gastro-intestinal tract. When chemo kills these cells, the blood quality diminishes, the hair falls out, and prolonged nausea occurs.

"I assume Dr. Grey has told you about the side effects of this chemo?"

"Oh, sure." I strove to respond valiantly. "There'll be some nausea, vomiting, maybe diarrhea. Also some loss of hair, possible cardiac damage from the Adriamycin, and then some general listlessness."

"Did he mention anything else?"

I tried to keep my mind off the slowly creeping liquid. "If so, I can't remember it." The Adriamycin seemed to hover about an inch above my wrist.

"What did he say about your sexual ability?"

"What?" I stammered.

At that moment the Adriamycin began trickling into my veins. My body jerked. I couldn't help but stare at my wrist.

"I don't remember anything about sex. Tell me really damn quickly so I can yank this tube out if necessary."

She laughed uncomfortably. Looking hesitatingly at me, she placed her hand back on my wrist.

"Well, your particular protocol will reduce your sperm count and its viability. This means two things. While you'll be able to have sex, you probably won't have much desire. There's also a possibility of permanent sterility. When used against breast cancer, Cytoxan has caused this sterility. But, we really don't know much about it."

She noticed my disbelief and tried to lessen the shock. "But there's a good side to this. Since you'll be sterile during chemo, you have a foolproof birthcontrol system if you do have sex." She giggled self-consciously and then continued. "We've often considered printing up an official medical certificate of sterility that our patients could use for whatever purposes they consider necessary."

I remember looking at her tanned face framed by her flowing blonde hair and believing that she might be the last woman I would be attracted to for a year. Quickly, however, the burning pain from the Adriamycin and especially the DTIC turned aside thoughts of a sexually abstemious year.

As the clear vial of DTIC emptied into my arm I temporarily felt overwhelmed. The tension from the last week, the marijuana, the two dozen brownies, and the drugs were battling each other for my attention. Pulling the needle from my arm, the chemotherapist congratulated me on my stoicism. I nodded my appreciation for her remark and smiled weakly.

"Is someone picking you up?" It was a statement more than a question.

I buttoned up my sleeve and slowly stood up.

"No. I'm taking the shuttle bus back to Harvard."

"Why didn't you ask a friend to come and get you?"

It was a difficult question to answer—self-reliance, desire not to bother friends (who likes to go to hospitals?), and a belief that friends' help is not inexhaustible and should be saved until absolutely necessary.

"I thought I wouldn't need them."

She drew in her breath and shook her head. "I wish you the best of luck. But next time, you dumb turkey, arrange to have somebody pick you up. I think you're going to start learning what friends can do."

But I walked carefully back to the bus and no problems arose. After all my preparation and listening to harrowing tales of chemo, I now surmised that I could conquer chemo and cancer. Even an hour of vomiting after supper could not dissuade me. My last thought as I climbed into bed was, "I can whip cancer."

After an early morning swim I impulsively telephoned Harvard's insurance office to confirm my assumption that Blue Cross-Blue Shield would cover all my radiation and chemotherapy costs. With a sinking feeling I heard the office manager relate that only employee insurance covered chemo. Student insurance did not.

"But I am an employee. The government department

pays me to teach and Dudley House provides room and board for me as a resident tutor. I'm getting the equivalent of $9,000 a year."

"Yes. However your primary function at Harvard is that of a student."

"The distinction is absurdly arbitrary," I replied, "and doctors tell me that chemo is necessary. How else can I ever pay for it?"

"Perhaps you have another private health plan?"

"No, I don't." I thought for a moment. "Tell me, how much does a single session of chemotherapy cost?"

She put me on hold while she rummaged through recent bulletins. At length she responded, "For your type of therapy, exclusive of hospitalization, the cost appears to be about six hundred dollars for two days. I'm sorry, but that's the way rules are and all of us have to live with them."

Totally exasperated and horrified, I hung up. How could I pay for such treatment? Should I take the treatment? And what if the chemo didn't work? I could not face death without completing the thesis. Every cancer patient needs goals to deter him from a passive, self-pitying life. Graduation was my major objective.

Remembrance of the recent paranoia prompted me on Wednesday not to use the remaining marijuana that Bill had provided. I felt tired and tense as I entered the chemo ward. The DTIC infusion continually burned my veins. My head began throbbing and a metallic taste spread throughout my mouth. As I finally rose from the chair my legs wobbled and, briefly, everything seemed to swim in front of me.

I set off once again to walk to the bus. The Sidney Farber Institute is a five-minute walk from the Deaconess. I felt exhausted upon reaching it. Everyone was moving faster than me and I regarded myself as a blundering obstacle slowly crossing their well-defined paths. A novice skier on an expert slope.

Fortunately, Longwood Avenue is downhill for one

block and then it levels off. I had fifteen minutes to walk three blocks. I wasn't sure that I could make it. At the corner of Blackfan and Longwood I looked about for a cab and quietly rejoiced that none appeared. This was a challenge, damn it, and I was going to beat it.

A block away from Pasteur Avenue I could see a handful of medical students scurrying towards an apparently full shuttle bus. I started running, laughing at the absurdity of my action. Another bus would be leaving in twenty minutes.

With a crunching of ancient gears, the bus slowly started moving; I reached out and frantically pounded on the doors. The driver gave me a resigned look and the doors wheezed open. I looked about. To my consternation, no seats were available. I was sandwiched in between three students, two of whom were smoking. I reached up for a rail and closed my eyes. Perhaps the trip would be shorter if I didn't watch.

The first inklings of a crisis occurred as the bus bumped over the inclined grates along the M.I.T. bridge that links Cambridge to Boston. Gastric liquid, the harbinger of nausea, began collecting in my mouth. I suddenly had an apparition of vomiting on the bus and cursed myself for not having asked Bob, or Debby, or Jon and Norah to drive me back.

Not only did rush hour traffic on Mass Ave seem interminable but the bus stopped more and more frequently to let off students. I felt alone and helpless as well as irritated at my penchant for self-reliance. While asking a friend to chauffeur me might be an inconvenience to him, vomiting on the shuttle bus would prove more than an inconvenience to a much larger number of people.

Finally the shuttle reached friendly lines; Lamont Library, the southeast corner of Harvard's kingdom. I insinuated myself between standing passengers and asked to be dropped at the corner of Holyoke Street.

Should I walk and not upset my stomach or should I

run? I ran. Fortunately my room key slipped easily into the keyhole and I quickly turned left into the bathroom. Out of control I bounced, like a top, first against one side and then against the other side of the bathroom door. Pushing myself into the bathroom I tripped over a plush Bloomingdale's throwrug and fell into the bathtub. Aided by Newton's Law, vomit was rushing up my throat. With a final effort I jerked up and found the toilet.

For half an hour I knelt and gazed at my lunch and, perhaps, I thought, several hundred dollars worth of chemicals which had taken leave of my system. Later I learned that in spite of my violent reactions, these chemicals don't in fact leave the system, as I assumed during my first few months of chemo. I vaguely remember the telephone ringing and someone knocking hesitatingly at my door, the knocks abruptly terminating upon my next coughing spasm.

Finally it was over. I slowly rose and made my way to the phone.

"Debby, it's me. I have chemo again in three weeks and I was wondering if I could reserve you as my driver."

Her reaction was immediate. "God damn you, Herb. What's been happening? I knocked on your door ten minutes ago and I heard obscene cadaverous grunts which I thought my Celtic literature had a monopoly on." She stopped to catch her breath. "Seriously, though, are you okay?"

I tersely related the recent happenings. Her reaction was "Oh, Jesus," followed by her hanging up the phone.

As I lay on the couch, consecutive burning and tingling waves surged through my body. "What the hell is going on?" I could not understand this unsettling pain. Usually I felt relief after vomiting. Now I realized that one attack would be followed by another, equally painful, seizure. Odd situations provoke odd thoughts. Yeats's "Second Coming" flashed into my mind: "Things fall apart; the center cannot hold; Mere anarchy is loosed upon the world."

I had reached home at five thirty. Two hours later I had made nine trips to the bathroom.

At eight o'clock Brian Duffy, a fellow tutor and neighbor, came by. With reddish brown hair, glowing cheeks, and a cherubic grin, Brian will always resemble an overgrown choirboy. He glanced inquiringly at me. "Debby says you've returned from chemotherapy." He smiled uncertainly. "You're feeling okay, aren't you?"

"Thanks, Brian. I was sick for a couple of hours, but it seems to be going away." I suddenly felt my stomach tighten and a taste of gastric juice in my mouth. While I deeply appreciated Brian's concern, his presence was somehow making me nervous.

Brian placed himself upon an ottoman, clasped his hands, and leaned in my direction. "Look, if I can be of any assistance, please let me know. You really won't be disturbing me. I'm just up two flights."

"Oh, God," I thought. "I really have to be alone." But I could not politely request him to leave. Fortunately, my physical system, once more in disarray, solved the dilemma. After he witnessed two prolonged vomiting seizures, Brian excused himself.

Ever since Debby had hung up the phone, she had been talking to other tutors in the building. Advising them of the situation, she emphasized that I tended to spurn offers of help unless they were forcibly and continually made. She now knocked on my open door, didn't hear a response, and entered.

"How are you doing, Herb?" she gently asked.

"Not too well, Deb. But I'm beginning to feel really tired and so I hope that the worst is over." I grinned weakly. "It's been quite a day."

"Sure there's nothing I can do?"

"Yup."

Debby looked at me for a long time. "I'll see you in the morning," she said finally upon leaving.

Only rarely did I know what effect my cancer was having upon other people. People who had close friends or relatives with cancer were among the most solicitous of my friends. Debby was deeply concerned not only because I was a very good friend but because she remembered vividly her own mother slowly dying of cancer ten years earlier.

After Debby left, her mission of mercy aborted, she scurried up the stairs looking for Brian.

"I was absolutely hysterical," Debby recalls. "I met Brian and burst into tears. Poor Brian, he had just left Barbie (another tutor) who was very distraught over your condition. Barbie's dad died of cancer when she was twelve and now both she and I were reliving our childhood anguish."

"Brian, what in God's name can we do about Herb? He's a pain in the ass and he won't ask for help."

Brian bit his lip and shook his head. "All I know is that he needs medical supervision. Herb needs to be mothered but he won't accept it."

"But, damn it, you've go to do something tonight; you saw him."

Brian returned to my room and exercised his bluff New York Irish charm. When I realized that he would not leave unless I came with him, I followed him to Stillman Infirmary where I spent the night.

The next morning I called Jon. I was irritated at myself for having given in to Brian. I wanted to fight cancer by myself, whereas a stay in Stillman was admitting that my body was losing the battle.

"Jon, I'm really up for some squash and I've got several free hours this afternoon."

Jon adamantly refused, citing Grey's warning that I should remain inactive for at least four days after each treatment. I walked over to Hemenway Gym where I encountered a scrawny mathematics graduate student.

"Easy game," I quickly deduced. But once on the court, this refugee from the logarithmic world sprinted successfully for my dropshots and backpedaled nimbly for my fol-

lowup lobs off the back wall. After my strong overhand
serve won the second game, my opponent excused himself.
Happily tired, I unfastened the Velcro glove grip and
headed toward the door. At that moment, a friend of mine
who had been watching from the stands came down and
challenged me to a set. I took the first game and then he
won the next four.

"Would you like to stop, Herb?"

But I was angry with my declining play and wanted to
contest at least one more game. Our next match was tied at
fourteen all so we went to extra points. He won, twenty-six
to twenty-four.

As I started my tennislike serve for the sixth game, the
racket slipped from my grasp, flew the length of the court,
and crashed against the front wall. My opponent looked at
me and somewhat nervously suggested that he was getting
tired and wanted to leave. "It's only a game," he said. After
agreeing to play in two days' time, we showered and left.
Though exhausted, I ran the last block home, had several
vomiting seizures in my bathroom, and then collapsed
upon the floor. At eleven that evening, Jon called. I briefly
recounted the afternoon's events and concluded "Life is
getting more complicated than I thought."

As fall inexorably progressed into winter, I noticed sev-
eral disquieting effects of C.A.D. Along with other Dudley
tutors, I lived in Apley Court, a five-story red brick building
built a hundred years ago. As part of Harvard's fabled "Gold
Coast," Apley has housed such future luminaries as Theo-
dore Roosevelt (whose valet lived across the hall in his own
suite). Unfortunately, Apley's heating and plumbing sys-
tem probably has not been revamped since young T.R.
frothed up San Juan Hill.

When the heat was turned off each night, the two pipes
next to my bed would begin an onerous clang that re-
minded one visitor of frenzied gnomes wielding hammers.
At six in the morning, when the heat was turned on, the
gnomes once more initiated their petulant pounding. If I

hadn't been going through cancer and chemo, the noise would have been tolerable. But with chemicals coursing through my system and thoughts of life and death, sexuality, family, insurance, and schoolwork running through my mind, the pipes prevented any prolonged sleep. Although pills were necessary for sleep, they kept me drowsy until midafternoon. Prior to that summer I never had a sleeping pill prescription. Now, because of my worries, the effects of C.A.D., and Apley's noisy pipes, I was allowing myself increasing dosages of Dalmane and Seconal.

Two weeks after my first chemo treatment I encountered another C.A.D. effect. On a Tuesday afternoon I was stalking the gym's heavy bag. Starting with short jabs, I began to move faster, flicking jabs, combinations and hooks, ducking, feinting, moving back, and then coming in again with renewed vigor.

After fifteen minutes I was wheezing and coughing. For some reason, I could not get enough air, even when I backed away from the bag.

"I can't believe it; something's in my throat."

I yanked off a speed glove and reached down my throat. To my utter amazement I pulled out a small pile of hair. Apparently I had been breathing heavily enough to suck them in. I threw the wad away and continued to slam the bag.

The next evening I was preparing to wrap up my class in Portland when my best student asked an insightful question. As she talked, I ruminatingly ran my hand through my hair. Suddenly my hand felt as if I had slipped a glove on. I stared at my hand. It was covered with hair. I quickly shoved my hirsute hand under some papers and answered the question. When I woke up the next morning, a formerly blue and white pillow was completely shaded with hair.

On December eighth I prepared for my second treatment. My white blood count, while having dropped from November's excellent 6,600, was judged adequate at 3,800. My alopecia (less politely, loss of hair) was so pronounced that I had reluctantly purchased a wig.

As Debby and Brian drove me home I remained largely silent, relieved that two good friends were helping me but unable to think about anything except the queasy and rapidly increasing warnings of nausea. Both hands gripping the wheel of her red Audi, Debby too remained silent as she strove, with only intermittent success, to dodge the potholes and bumps which grace Boston's back streets.

Brian broke an awkward silence. "How are you feeling, Herb?"

I looked at Brian. My only thought was of getting home and vomiting as soon as possible.

"I think I'll be okay when I get back to Apley" was all I could say.

Brian glanced at Debby. "Look, Herb, we're really happy to help. Even Ali needs a cornerman. Well, we're your cornerman and we're staying with you for the distance."

Suddenly the Audi slammed into a chasmic pothole. I doubled over. Brian reached towards me. "Hey, man, are you okay?"

I slowly peered up at a concerned Brian. "Chemo ain't so bad," I announced. "It stimulates the natural impulses. I'm gonna get back at four o'clock and puke my guts out in front of the Mike Douglas Show." Debby burst into a prolonged bray and Brian, visibly relieved, said, "Hey, we don't have anything to worry about with you."

The vomiting attacks were more insistent and prolonged than three weeks earlier. When they ended at nine thirty, I propped myself against the bathtub and slowly started sobbing. Six months, I reckoned, could be a very long time. An hour later I reluctantly admitted myself to Stillman for the night.

Declining Debby's offer to drive on Thursday, I called up a close friend and former roommate of mine. Bob and I had been alike in a number of ways. We had played the same sports together, sometimes dated each other's old girlfriends, and received equally high academic marks. I had been surprised that Bob had not called for several weeks. Somewhat reluctantly, he agreed to stop by at four o'clock to pick me up.

A major drawback of intravenous chemotherapy is that the second day's dosage is infinitely more painful than the first day's. The patient remains physically weak from the preceding day and displays a lowered tolerance for pain. A nurse once confided to me, "It's on the second day when nurses feel frustrated that we can't reach out to the patient and somehow give him our understanding and affection. It's a pleasant wonder that so many kids or older people in their sixties keep coming in when they know what pain they'll receive." As Dr. Grey had counseled me earlier, "Each time you'll feel worse. Expect it and try to take it in stride."

Now, on Thursday afternoon, I was gripping my wrist as the Andriamycin flowed in. The burning was rapidly becoming unbearable. Painful tinglings scratched inside my fingers and toes. I finally looked up at the chemotherapist and asked her to slow the pace. She adjusted the flow valve, glanced at me, and asked, "Is someone picking you up again today?"

I was encountering difficulty pushing the sleeve button through the buttonhole. Everything appeared slightly out of focus and I felt weak, almost woozy. I looked up at her.

"Yes," I grinned concedingly. "I guess I learnt my lesson."

The Adriamycin alone had taken fifteen minutes. Increasingly I requested the chemotherapist to decrease the flow. I was slouching staring at the floor. I dimly noticed that Bob was standing in the door with an amazed and pained expression. When I caught his attention he averted his eyes and continued staring at the IV system and my wrist.

After my very first chemo session, I had strolled half a mile to the bus; this time a nurse carefully maneuvered me into a wheelchair and piloted me slowly down the halls to the underground parking lot.

Bob, who had not spoken since arriving some thirty

minutes before, vacantly commented, "Jeez, I didn't think it was this bad." He helped me into the car and began driving.

"How much longer will you be going through this?"

"Apparently six months."

"Well, I don't know if I can get out of work again by four to pick you up. You know that I'd like to, Herb, but they're hitting us junior lawyers with a shitload of work."

I nodded dutifully and inquired about his squash game. He warmed to the subject and held forth about his progress up the various ladders of competition at the Harvard Club. Capturing him in his glow, I arranged a squash date for the next week.

The admittance report and followup observations recorded pernicious vomiting and diarrhea as I spent the evening in Stillman. Lying in bed, I bitterly realized that I had a low threshold of pain. My stoicism became increasingly forced each time the drugs snaked through my veins or when my stomach muscles protested after a five-hour period of vomiting.

Staring at the ceiling, I conceded that my living habits also lessened my physical resistance. Apley's pipes continued their cacophony through the nights. Harvard's Buildings and Grounds commiserated but noted that they could not attend to it until late spring. Another problem was that I had no present girlfriend. Since I felt little sexual desire, I felt a certain trepidation at starting a relationship. My September attempts had floundered when I told the women that I was going through cancer treatments. Personal rejection at this stage was the last thing I needed. Finally, Conant had been suggesting that sports were lessening my resistance by contributing to my insomnia.

Chemo was also making me tense by increasing my passivity. My life was at stake, yet since I knew nothing about mitosis, metastisization, and a thousand other processes, I had to defer to my doctors. The chemotherapy induced ennui. "Damn it," I thought. "More and more I know what I want because cancer has forced me to re-examine my life. Yet chemo is preventing me from realizing the new goals." Paradoxically, the disease of cancer had proved, in part, to be a blessing in disguise whereas the disease's possible cure was destroying many of life's joys.

As I lay in Stillman on Thursday, a nurse glided through the darkness to my bed, her white dress appearing as a gray death shroud in the darkness.

"Mr. Howe, are you awake?"

I blinked away my self-pitying thoughts. She smiled and said, "You see, I was sent to give you a sleeping injection and I knew that I'd have to ask you to roll over." She hesitated. "I guess it's kind of stupid to wake you up for that." I did not reply but a grin of great contentment spread over my face. I remembered soggy towels, safety belts, and "union policy." Bureaucratic intransigence had unconsciously provided invaluable comic relief. The world no longer seemed so impossible. I rolled over and vaguely felt a pinprick as I fell asleep.

For the first two days after my December chemo treatment I did nothing but lie on my sofa, hold court with visiting friends, and eat. Jane continually indulged my distinctly nonepicurean taste for chocolate ice cream with salted peanuts. By Sunday I grew so angry at my passivity that I telephoned an acquaintance who knew nothing about my chemotherapy.

Danny, as befits most Harvard law students, possesses a massively competitive spirit. We jogged down Holyoke Street, past the colonial residence of Professor John Fairbanks, and through the Dunster courtyard to the Charles River. I glanced at my running partner; I was ready.

"What's our target?" I asked.

Danny sonorously blew his nose and shook his head like a racehorse chafing at the bit. "Let's try for the M.I.T. boathouse. I've never done it." The boathouse lay about three miles down the Charles River.

The run from Harvard along the grass paralleling Memorial Drive into Boston offers innumerable small delights. You pass groups of runners displaying myriad shapes and styles who, regardless of their present breathing pattern, will invariably greet you with an abbreviated "hello" or, at the very least, a friendly nod. White sailing dinghies with sails of yellow, red, white, or blue bounce upon a wind-churned Charles. By five in the evening a mellowing red sun is setting behind the John Hancock building, whose modern glass structure mirrors Trinity Church, built in the mid-1800's. Rather than numbing a runner along the Charles, a December offshore wind invigorates his senses.

Having reached Western Avenue, half the distance to the M.I.T. boathouse, I looked at Danny. We had been running at a rapid four-fifths speed. Sweat trickled across a beet-red face. His breathing sounded hoarse and heavy, like a truck in first gear.

"I'm feeling pain," I thought, "but I wonder if I can beat this healthy human. Certainly won't know unless I try." We kept running, oblivious of passers-by and of our own pain. We sprinted the last twenty yards to the boathouse and, as Danny grunted recognition of our accomplishment, we turned around and silently started back.

At Winthrop House my right knee suddenly buckled. Off balance, I pitched to my right and stuck a large iron fence. I fell onto the sidewalk.

Danny looked around; the run was nearly over. "Are you okay?"

I replied, "Yeah, I just tripped" and we jogged the remaining few blocks to the Indoor Athletic Building. As I walked home I broadly smiled. Physically, I felt exhilarated by the warm rush of blood through my body on that cold December day. Mentally, I was wide awake. I had overcome what seemed an insurmountable obstacle: almost six miles of hard running three days after chemotherapy. "If I can do this," I reflected, "maybe I can finish chemo's six months."

But, each night I fought the pipes and each night the pipes won. Worrying that I might become addicted to Seconal, Dr. Conant had placed me on Dalmane. I was averaging over forty milligrams of Dalmane every night.

Since I usually felt either sleepy or drugged, school-work was increasingly difficult to finish. By mid-December I had not completed any of the four thesis chapters which I had promised Professor Kilson for December first. Assuming that chemo would grow increasingly arduous and that each recovery time would become longer, I calculated that I had only two months to write, rewrite, and then type a three-hundred-page tome. Since learning that I might die, a June graduation was paramount. It seemed impossible to continue chemo and to get my Ph.D. in June. I had to stop my chemo treatments.

Refusing to admit a complete defeat, I took solace in the view that finishing the thesis constituted more of a victory than passively enduring the chemotherapy. Time was precious and something to enjoy, rather than passively endure.

Shortly before Christmas vacation, I called on Dr. Grey at the Deaconess. While waiting for him, I talked to a hospital social worker. As I later discovered, her report concluded that I had "been an independent and successful individual who for the first time is coming up against a situation wherein he is placed in a dependent role to an extent he has not previously experienced. Financial pressures seem to be major factors for him at this time . . . He has discovered that his Blue Cross-Blue Shield student plan does not cover the cost of radiation therapy and chemotherapy . . . he is very anxious to complete (t)his Ph.D. work so that he may graduate in June . . . With all these pressures plus his current diminished physical reservoir, the patient does appear to have resilient personality strengths and sufficient coping ability."

Sufficient coping ability? As I watched Dr. Grey read my file, I felt woefully inadequate to cope with any more chemotherapy. At length, Dr. Grey looked up and in his quiet, confident voice asked how I felt.

I had my speech prepared. "The chemo is presenting me with several serious problems. No one has any idea of how long I'm going to live. They shade their confidence with qualifications and uncertainties. As I may have mentioned previously, there's only one certainty in my life. I desperately want to finish my thesis within the next two months. Chemo is preventing me from doing this. If I do die soon, I need a justification for all my years in graduate school."

Dr. Grey considered my outburst. He walked to his window and looked out. The first snow of the season was falling from Cambridge's gray skies.

I hesitated. When I was young, my motto had been "Never give up." As a result I had received two broken arms and innumerable bloody noses. Now I was requesting a strategic withdrawal.

"I'd like to discontinue chemo for three months so I may resume a regular writing and teaching schedule. By March I will have typed a final rough draft and I can pay a professional typist for the final draft. Then, I'll be very happy to come back for the remainder of the treatments."

Dr. Grey's mouth tightened as he watched the increasing snow swirl between the hospital buildings. "Is he ever going to reply?" I wondered.

Still standing at the window, he finally commented, "It's not as easy as that. First of all, the chemo may take much longer than six months. Perhaps, two and a half years."

"All I'm asking for is a three-month pause in the protocol. I do believe in taking chemo. With the thesis completed I'll be less tense and chemo will be much easier." The revelation of two and a half years of chemo and its costs had not yet sunk in.

He swung around. "Time is of the utmost importance. We have to pump as much of the Cytoxan, Adriamycin, and DTIC into you as quickly as possible."

"But three months. Am I asking very much?"

He looked at me for a long time. "I'll be blunt," he replied. "You have a choice of three hundred days to live or thirteen thousand days. It's your choice."

# Four

TWO DAYS AFTER talking with Dr. Grey I left Cambridge to spend Christmas with Lin and her family in Cooperstown, New York.

No major roads connect Cooperstown with the rest of New York and, except for farming, the town has no major industry. More than most American towns, Cooperstown proudly asserts its traditions. The father of James Fenimore Cooper established Cooperstown and Cooper's *Deerslayer* is set in the Cooperstown area of the 1760's. With less than twenty-five-hundred residents, Cooperstown has seven museums; Farmers' Museum, which is the largest, covers twenty acres. With its quiet pace, its hills, forests, and lakes, Cooperstown offered relief from the tension that had been building in Cambridge. Cooperstown also offered my nieces and nephews.

Vinia, Willie, and Johnnie had provided in Bristol a welcome antidote from the burgeoning worries about cancer. As I progressed through radiation and chemo, I realized how much I needed such diversions as kids, music, and sports.

Vinia, Willie, and John offered me an excuse to discard adult pretensions and once more act as a child. Because of Vinia and Co., I had begun a game at Thanksgiving that was as enjoyable as it was absurd. Lin had told them that my illness might have changed my appearance. Before I joined them for Thanksgiving in Cooperstown they called to ask whether they would be able to recognize me. This gave me an idea.

On my way to the bus station I stopped off at a novelty store near the Boston Commons to check out their selection of masks. Bypassing a Dracula who was grinning idiotically despite (or, perhaps, because of) a stake driven through his plastic head, I settled for a more subdued representative from the Planet of the Apes. As the bus pulled into the Albany terminal, where Lin had agreed to pick me up, I reached into my suitcase and extracted my Look Nouveau. The terminal was crammed with Thanksgiving travellers—an equal mix of college students and grandmothers with tinted hair. As I walked through the terminal an elderly woman in a blue pantsuit screamed, recovered herself, and then giggled nonstop. Mothers reined in their staring children and college students grinned as I moved towards Vinia, Willie, and John who were searching for their cancer-stricken uncle. Johnnie, buried in a green snowsuit, saw me first. He stared uncomprehendingly, slowly shaking his head in disbelief. Then as recognition flooded his face, he screamed delightedly and ran towards me. "That's my uncle, that's my uncle" he yelled to nobody—and thus, everybody—in particular.

My disguises soon became an expected custom. Ape-Face gave way to rubber noses, bushy eyebrows, and thick glasses which in turn were superseded by a nefarious pirate character whose twisted snarl fetchingly displayed his two remaining front teeth. I had started wearing the masks as a joke, but I soon realized that other people saw the masks as an indication that I could still laugh at some aspects of having cancer and chemotherapy. When I once wore a mask to Senior Common Room lunch, Debbie said, "This certifies to us that you're a nut. But at least we're more comfortable with you this way than if you were the typical, withdrawn, self-pitying sicko." The commiseration of doctors and friends over my loss of hair was as misplaced as it was well-intentioned. The wig soon created essential humor. Shortly before leaving Cambridge for Christmas I had dinner with Steve Cohen and his parents. In my class on "Revolution" last year, Steve had been my best student and we had become good friends. Now, the night before Hanukkah, the Cohens and I were standing around a Jewish menorah and preparing to light the candles. Suddenly Mrs. Cohen realized that they did not have an extra yarmulke for me. As they wondered what to do, I doffed my wig. "Is this a reasonable facsimile?" I asked. Dr. Cohen, while readily acknowledging his shortcomings as a Talmudic scholar, replied in the affirmative. The ceremony continued.

And now, as I arrived in Cooperstown for Christmas vacation, I realized that I hadn't brought any new disguises. Despite my midnight arrival, Willie was determined to see if his uncle had changed in the last month. As I wearily trudged through the kitchen and into the living room, Willie looked up from behind the sofa where he had been playing with his guinea pigs.

"Hi, Uncle Herbie," he diplomatically greeted me. "Let's see your bald head and wig."

Dutifully I took off my skicap and tossed him the wig. Lin and I talked for another half hour and then I retired to bed. Waking up late next morning, I remembered that Willie had appropriated my wig. I clumped downstairs and eventually found Willie in the backyard where he was busily constructing his latest snow fort.

"Oh, your wig? Sure, I've got it. But, Uncle Herbie . . ." He paused, uncertainly. "May I keep your wig?"

I asked him why.

"My guinea pigs love it—they think it's a great nest."

Having visions of smelly rodents nibbling at my expensive hairpiece, I half-pushed, half-followed my nephew to the back of the couch. His chirping guinea pigs indeed were rolling about in a now stained and misshapen hair-piece. My anger rapidly turned into a grudging admiration of my nephew since he was following in family footsteps: I knew that if given the chance I probably would have done the same thing at his age. Willie and I declared a truce and I took my wig to a rather bemused drycleaner who confessed wigs had never been his specialty.

On Thursday, two days before Christmas, I walked down the Payson's driveway with Boogie, the family beagle. It was late in the afternoon, snowing, and I knew that in half an hour it would be dark. I paused when I heard Lin yelling. She ran up to me, pulling a heavy sweater over her head.

"Herb," she began, "you've been here for two days but you've been so caught up with my kids that you and I haven't talked very much."

I had never felt close to Lin. Two years older than me, she had skipped two grades in school and gone on to Radcliffe at sixteen. Meanwhile, I was embarrassing my parents with decidedly nonacademic behavior.

I trace my early distaste for academics and my feelings about Lin to our first sibling confrontation. When I was one year old, lying in the playpen and definitely minding my own business, I was suddenly set upon by three-year-old Lin who, armed with a broomstick, did her best to poke out my eye. I rolled about but clearly was no match for this older woman with a broom. I screamed and, to Lin's chagrin, was rescued by my parents.

The incident showed me the pitfalls of a classical education. My parents had unconsciously provoked my sister by reading the story of how Ulysses rescued himself and his men from Polyphemus, the Cyclops, by driving a stake through his one eye. Impressionable Linnet mistook her brother for Polyphemus.

While she delighted her parents later with academic honors, I enjoyed sports and, as my third grade teacher recorded, had "a fine but mischievous character." That year I had incurred the wrath of my school's principal by emptying my marble collection from the back of the auditorium while the rest of the school suffered through that classic film, "Rice Growing in the Andes."

I had the unenviable task of following my sister's academic achievements. I had an uneasy feeling that my parents wrote me off when, as a junior in high school, I slunk home with my report card displaying an "F" in Latin. My father, who happened to be Chairman of the Classics Department at the University of Wisconsin, was not overly amused. I later began receiving better grades, yet our divergent childhoods prevented me from becoming close to Lin.

As we walked down Beaver Street I detailed to Lin how Apley's pipes, my preoccupation with completing school, and the numerous worries and effects of cancer and chemotherapy had prompted me to postpone the treatments and how Grey had reacted to my decision.

When I had finished, Lin nodded silently and kept walking. The snow, which had started falling at lunchtime, was quickly increasing. I looked at Lin and waited for her response. I knew better than to ask her opinion immediately. My sister has a logical mind. She considers each piece of information and weighs questions, alternatives, and solutions before speaking.

"As I see it, you have two choices," she finally replied. "And each has its risks. A: stop the chemo until you've finished the thesis. The problem, of course, is that without chemo you might die, possibly even before you complete the doctorate. Yet B isn't much better. If you stay with chemo, things'll probably get worse. And you might do the thesis for only a few hours a week before eventually becoming a vegetable."

"You're my brother but I don't know you very well. One thing I do know is that you want to feel active and that you're progressing. And maybe keeping on with chemo won't give you that feeling. But Herbie, you do belong to something called a family. And, while we'll support whatever you decide, we want you to keep going with the treatments. Not graduating this year seems like such a short-run loss when compared with dying."

Lin raised her hand, indicating that she hadn't finished. "Okay, maybe the chemo's bad for you or maybe it's just ineffective. Completing the Ph.D. would satisfy your pride, and you do need that now. But damn it, brother, we're talking about life and death."

Lin paused and studied me. The heavy snowfall was muffling all nearby sounds, even the shrieks of kids sledding down the slope near Bassett Hospital.

"Isn't this really a matter of pride?" she asked. "I mean, aren't you giving up and taking the easy way out? Wouldn't continuing chemo be the bigger challenge and bigger accomplishment? If you are going to die, wouldn't it still be more satisfying to have pushed yourself to the limit physically and mentally, rather than wasting away in your Harvard office writing about an African political event that no longer appears important?"

The drifts leading down to Otsego lake were insurmountable so we walked past the Carriage Museum and the Baseball Hall of Fame, where the outdoor scoreboard still gave the particulars of October's last World Series game. We walked on to Star Meadow, where Vinia, Willie, John, and I had played hide-and-go-seek during summer vacations. By seven o'clock we returned home. While I hadn't resolved anything, I now felt a deeper appreciation for my sister. She had joined other friends of mine who would discuss my cancer and offer suggestions rather than pity. After amusing Vinia with how I won my Boy Scout cooking merit badge (fried onions and maple syrup) and how I had caught my first fish (unfortunately, I had placed the line between the slats of the pier and couldn't unhook the unlucky perch), I contentedly fell asleep.

For the rest of Christmas vacation, Cooperstown allowed me to step away from the immediate pressures of Cambridge. I spent endless hours sledding with Vinia and Co. behind Bassett Hospital on the hills we christened

"Heartbreak" and "Super-Suicide." On Monday we started at three in the afternoon and stopped six hours later. The crisp air and bright moonlight drove all thoughts of Cambridge from my mind.

As one of us would attempt something new, such as lying backwards on the sled and thus sacrificing any control, the others would follow in turn. I had thought that Johnnie, being the youngest, would bellow when smashing up or falling off, but instead he gurgled contentedly, collected his dented sled, and trudged happily up the hill.

On Christmas Eve I attended church with Lin and the children while Charlie assisted the rector, Father French, with the service. As the choir trooped in during the processional I couldn't help but notice Vinia watching me intently. I peered down at her. With an impish grin she quickly looked away and attempted to find the correct passage in the hymnal.

A few minutes later, during the reading of the first lesson I again felt her gaze. Finally, when Father French said "we should count all our blessings from this year," I turned to Vinia.

"Why do you keep staring at me?" I asked.

"I'm bored and so I'm waiting to see your wig fall off," she responded.

For the first Christmas in several years I truly felt part of a family, as all of us sprawled around the Christmas tree and opened presents. My hair, or lack of it, was duly observed. Several relatives had knitted skicaps for the Cambridge winter. And Willie, with a sly grin, passed me a small, elaborately wrapped package. "It's something all of us like," he chortled, "but I'm giving it to you because I know that you really can't part with it." He had given me a twenty-nine-cent comb.

After brunch Willie, Vinia, and Johnnie bundled up and trooped outside to compare loot with their friends. When they returned, they woke me up and told me I had been chosen captain of their backyard football game.

It was still snowing and bitterly cold as I barked out signals and threw pass after pass to Willie who, despite his cold hands and skinny build, would catch the ball and run directly at the larger, defensive ends. Whenever he was knocked down, he doggedly insisted that he wasn't hurt and that "we've just got to win."

I had been wearing the skicap rather than the wig. But after one series of downs, in which the entire defensive line buried me deeper into the snow, I lost the skicap. Shortly before the game ended, a neighbor called Vinia over to a kitchen doorway.

"What's the matter with your uncle?" she inquired. "At church yesterday he had a full head of hair. But now, he's got nothing."

"Oh, that?" replied Vinia. "Uncle Herbie's had a hysterectomy."

Breakfast on the twenty-sixth was marked by Willie surreptitiously putting Tabasco sauce into Johnnie's corn-flakes. As Johnnie, red-faced with tears streaming down his cheeks, chugged indignantly after his fleeing brother, I stretched contentedly on the sofa. Cambridge seemed far away while I read Michael Crichton's escapist *Great Train Robbery* about the seamier aspects of Victorian London.

Charlie soon sat down nearby. After joking about Vinia's medical diagnostic abilities, my brother-in-law asked whether cancer had changed my agnostic beliefs. Going to church still offered me little comfort, but, while I hadn't prayed to God, I could more clearly see the benefits of religion.

I told him of imagining Johnnie asking if he'd ever see me again once I died. "The whole notion of an afterlife," I told Charlie, "is comforting. It's like Donne's poem, 'Death Be Not Proud,' where death is a short bridge between the present and the future. Eventually everyone crosses it and meets again on the other side."

Charlie nodded. Amidst upstairs accusations of "you did

so," "I did not," and "I'm telling Mom," Charlie wondered
whether I now believed there may be a God. "If there isn't,"
I replied, "it makes no sense in believing there is. And if he
does exist, I hope he'll pay more attention to my activities
rather than prayers; actions, as it were, rather than words."

"Most of all, I want to control what's happening. I guess
it's for my own ego. But I've got to fight cancer by myself." I
looked at Charlie. "Yet I'm stymied. I don't know how to do
it. I've stopped eating salt and candy and I've been drinking
a lot of vegetable juices. But that's not really going to help
me much."

On my last evening, John and Willie and Vinia had
changed into pajamas and were lounging contentedly in
front of the fireplace. As the sounds of Beethoven's "Ninth
Symphony" filled the room, I looked up from a magazine
and watched the kids make s'mores (marshmallows, Gra-
ham crackers, and chocolate). However temporary, every-
thing appeared idyllic. I had always assumed that I would
someday raise a family, Now, with the cancer and my
chemo decision, that assumption had become a lost dream.

After clearing my bed of rubber snakes, I slept well and
woke early the next morning to begin packing. As we drove
to the Albany bus station, and as Willie continued his rap-
idly wearing litany of baldness jokes, I thanked Lin and
Charlie for their hospitality.

I had considered the discussion with Lin. Taking
chemo did come down to a question of life or death. In
Cooperstown the physical pain of chemo, the mental
anguish over the pipes, my listlessness, my impotence, and
my thesis appeared trivial. Reluctantly I concurred that
continuing chemo was a challenge. A few months earlier
Claudia had encouraged me to do as much as possible as
quickly as possible. Now I had my chance.

My upbeat mood persisted in Cambridge. Conant and
my friends applauded my decision and I was buoyed by the
traditional optimism and determination that marks the new

year's beginning. I prided myself on my new determina-
tion—cancer might be a mysterious dread to others but to
me it now appeared as a fallible enemy backed up against
the ropes.

Every Thursday that year I walked to the residence of
the Master of Dudley House for tea. Although all tutors
were expected to attend, I enjoyed the occasion and went
willingly. As faculty, tutors, and students are thrown
together with beer and brandy, sandwiches and tea, they
rediscover that Harvard can be a society of learned men
and women and not simply an academic gladiatorial pit
where gradegrubbing/lazy/radical/apathetic/irreverent stu-
dents do battle against paleolithic/liberal/senile/irrelevant
professors.

On my first Thursday back I had just finished talking
with Debbie and Norah about Cooperstown when a middle-
aged administrator sidled up to me and bluntly asked if I
was the tutor who had fatal cancer. Taken aback, I said yes.
He looked at me intently. "God," he said, "it must be
rough" and promptly excused himself to get another drink.
He did not return.

Later, as I walked the two blocks over to Lowell House
for dinner, I thought about the administrator's conclusion.
Why didn't I feel pathetically hopeless, a human vegetable
faced with a bleak future of quick death or dependence
upon drugs? The sacrifices extorted by cancer were obvi-
ous, but saving graces were equally present.

Dramatic images from recent movies and books about
cancer came to mind. Young Johnny Gunther with his
head swathed in bandages as he struggled to finish his last
year at Deerfield Academy. His fragility paradoxically
pointed up his resilience and strength. An old TV docu-
mentary about *Life* photographer Margaret Bourke-White
and how she proudly resisted any self-pity after a brain
operation. And Brian Piccolo in the more recent *Brian's
Song* and how, with the aid of football and athletics, he had
waged a valiant struggle against cancer. I was not a star

athlete or journalist. But I did have a very rare form of cancer and this rarity added to the drama. I knew that doctors across the nation were following my progress; I was not just another cancer patient. And, like all other cancer patients, I was confronting the challenge of my life.

When I had first read *Death Be Not Proud* or seen the TV movies, I had been patronizingly glib about the pathos. But as I walked into Lowell House I thought that my situation was equally dramatic. "It's life and death. I've got a chance to see how really good I might be." I imagined a movie camera hovering above me; the drama of cancer was now outweighing the tragedy and self-pity.

I felt supremely confident of my mastery over chemo on the day before the next session. Late that afternoon I played two hard hours of squash and left the court grinning, sopping with sweat. As I was dressing in the locker room, a radio was playing "The First Noel." I looked up and noticed that everyone was quiet, still, as if frozen in a photograph. It was one of those rare moments when everything appears subdued and perfect. Outside, a soft snow fell as I strolled home. As I gazed at the stars I felt joyful about being alive and able to push myself beyond my fears.

Many chemotherapy patients adopt rituals to alleviate the inevitable fears just before a chemo session. On the last weekday before chemo I would work hard at my thesis, usually by finishing another draft of a chapter, and thus have no angst about how chemo was slowing my work. On the day of chemo I would read the morning *Globe* and concentrate on the personal interest and "crazies" stories ("Dead Horse Wins California Primary"). After chatting with fellow dissertation writers, most of whom welcomed yet another excuse to refrain from writing, I would have a light swim and then walk along the Charles or through the Yard.

At eleven o'clock on Wednesday morning I went swimming, then talked to Professor Williams afterwards in the lockerroom. I had become good friends with Williams and his wife, Paula. Williams knew that I was doing chemo in the afternoon but kept the conversation on gossip about faculty members or the declining fortunes of the Boston Celtics.

Returning to Apley, I picked up a recent letter from my parents in Madison; they had been writing weekly for the past two months. After announcing that Emily was pregnant, they inquired whether chemo was easier to take. "Not really," I thought, "but I'll get through it."

At the letter's end my mother noted, "You've always been an independent sort about physical pain—do you remember walking up from Randall School, coming in the house and telling me matter-of-factly, 'Mom, I broke my arm. I gotta go to the hospital?' You've never been the type to run to Momma, wanting your hand held. But isn't cancer different? For heaven's sake if it is, tell us. Either come out here—stay with us or Emily—or else we'll be happy to hop a plane. But write! Much luv, Muv."

During the last months I had become increasingly drawn to my family. Yet this was my struggle. I knew that I would fear cancer (and chemo) less if I could pull something useful from the experience. I wanted to know how far I could go it alone. Because I already depended heavily upon the medical profession, I needed to be in charge of some of my own battles. I appreciated my parents' offer but knew that I would not return to Madison.

Since I'd be staying overnight for my next treatment, I continued the ritualization in my suite at Apley by gathering up my electric blanket, my radio, and a trashy magazine that predicted the astrological fortunes of aging Hollywood stars. Such personal property permitted the illusion that I was controlling my hospital environment.

I smiled contentedly at my thesis. On Tuesday I had finished the first two chapters. I had labored for two months on this difficult theoretical section and now I felt equal shares of relief and pride at having finished it. Snow was falling heavily as I crossed Holyoke Street and entered Stillman.

As a young nurse assembled the IV tree and arranged

the drug vials, Dr. Conant sat on the edge of the bed and tried to divert my attention. More than most doctors, Loring realized the need to put a patient at ease to earn his trust and loyalty. When he inquired about my vacation, I rattled on about Cooperstown and the kids. Loring, who has two young children, smiled knowingly and said nothing.

As the nurse watched, Conant quickly injected the Cytoxan. I began to feel pain and dizziness only during the last few minutes of the DTIC. As I stared vacantly at the falling snow I suddenly had a fleeting image of a large translucent cancer cell being budged by a water current and then, with a "whoosh," being sucked down a large drain. I didn't say anything, but quietly I exulted "I've made it—I've beaten the chemo and the chemo's beaten cancer." I thanked Lin, her kids, and such friends as Jon and Janie who steadfastly urged the need for continued chemo.

The chemo had taken only fifteen minutes. As Conant left he remarked, "Vinia's diagnosis makes her a prime candidate for Harvard Med School." I smiled, said that I'd see him tomorrow, and then picked up *People* magazine.

The snow was amusing itself with rush hour traffic. I put down *People* and gimpily walked to a chair by the bay window. Pulling a blanket up to my waist I rang the nurses' station for a pitcher of ginger ale and a tray of cookies. Outside was a magnificent two-block spectacle of cars slamming on their brakes around J. Press clothing store, skidding past the Signet and Fly clubs, and then thumping into already stranded vehicles outside the Harvard Lampoon and Quincy House. I sipped the ginger ale and ate a handful of cookies. Outside, technology was meeting its match. A few hours later, after several prolonged periods of vomiting my breakfast, the ginger ale, and the cookies, I fell asleep.

When Conant came in the next morning, he agreed that I could leave for several hours as long as I returned by two that afternoon. As I walked past the crowded bookstores on Mass Ave I munched a rocky road ice cream cone and studied the red-faced, contented undergraduates. Six months ago I had considered myself just another student. Now they seemed so naive, innocent, and unprepared for life's later misfortunes. I smiled at the small library of books cradled in their arms. I reflected that while I had become an expert in African politics and had read Rousseau, Mill, Weber, and Marx, none of my university years had trained me for what I was now going through. Harvard was giving me, now, a more important education than I had ever previously received.

Conant handled the chemotherapy as he had on Tuesday. But a rapid chill spread through my body. I turned the blanket's heat control from "3" to "maximum" without feeling any warmer. Just as the DTIC was injected, I reluctantly asked Loring to halt the flow temporarily.

But soon the pain became insufferable. My body started shaking from the cold and tears rolled down my cheeks. Loring looked up inquiringly, but I shook my head. I wasn't going to halt the flow.

Soon my arm felt as if it was burning. Involuntarily I started coughing. Mucus dribbled from my nose. The nurse was staring at me while Loring fixed his eyes on the flow, undoubtedly hoping that it would go faster.

The trick is not to watch the vials—chemo seemed to proceed more slowly when watched. I glanced at *People* magazine where Charlie's Angels graced the cover. Perhaps Kate's all-knowing smile, Jaclyn's compassionate eyes and Farrah's hungry lustiness could pull me through. I hardly noticed the nurse wipe my eyes and my nose.

Finally, we made it. Loring smiled at me and began disassembling the tubing. In quiet appreciation I took one last look at the Angels. Loring patted my shoulder and bent over the washbasin to rinse off his hands. I swilled ginger ale inside my mouth to lessen the metallic taste.

After a few minutes I noticed that Loring was still hunched over the washbasin and that the water was still running. The nurse was staring uncertainly at Conant.

Finally as Loring turned around he forced a half-smile

and looked at me. "Herb, there're some times I don't enjoy my profession, such as when I administer pain to patients I especially like and see the effect that it's having on them. Being a doctor, I usually know that I'm helping people. But in your case, I walk in at two o'clock and I see a fairly healthy individual. Then, in an hour, you're obviously in pain and looking downright awful." Grinning more fully, Loring concluded, "Thanks a lot, you turkey." He laughed and said he'd see me the next day.

Five minutes later my teeth started chattering and I suddenly felt very dizzy. My stomach convulsed and a stream of vomit shot from my mouth and onto the sheets. I looked for the green basin. I couldn't see it. I threw myself off the bed and groped towards the bathroom. Almost there, and then an uncontrollable burst of diarrhea. As I felt it trickle between my legs I once more vomited.

I grabbed the toilet with both hands and closed my eyes as I continued to vomit. The taste and the smell of the vomit was terrible. Finally, too weak to move back to bed, I eased myself onto the cold, tiled floor of the bathroom. I glanced around. My hospital gown was stained and the floor around the bathroom and leading to my bed was a vile, reddish-brown color. As the pain in my sides subsided, I pulled myself up and wearily limped back to bed, where I called for an orderly to get a new gown and to clean the floor.

Angry and stunned, I lay in bed, amazed at how quickly the chemotherapy had overpowered me. Clearly I hadn't lived up to my friends' expectations and encouragement. I thought of the past three weeks, of Cooperstown, of Jon, Norah, and Jane, and of the chimerical belief that I had willed myself over chemo.

"Fuckin' world; nothing's changed." I angrily bit my lip and tried to sleep. Three hours later, after 100 milligrams of Seconal, I succeeded.

As a breakfast nurse slid the tray towards me she asked if I wanted to remain in Stillman for another day. I thought for a moment. I needed to demonstrate that I could still control my life. To the nurse I nodded my appreciation but mentioned that I felt okay, just a little tired.

Shortly thereafter Dr. Conant walked in and, seeing an undoubtedly distressed face, said "I guess it didn't go so well." I offered a weak grin. I had long since discarded the stoical, good patient pretense when talking to Loring. I told him about the vomiting, the diarrhea, and my worries about chemo's effects.

"I hope you're continuing our protocol," Conant gently said.

I looked out the window. From past experience I knew that my hatred of chemo peaked during and shortly after the treatments. About two weeks after each treatment I would grudgingly resign myself to more chemo. And, as Lin had noted, the final consideration was that of life or death. I nodded my assent.

Conant smiled with relief. He paused at the door. "I know you like to leave here in a hurry but you're looking unusually tired. Take it easy, okay?"

I showered and thumbed through the mail at Apley. Another Blue Cross bill for a thousand dollars, a reminder from the government department that graduating Ph.D. students must turn in their theses by April 15th, and a letter announcing the death of my Uncle Pete.

A singular joy of youth is when an idolized adult treats a child as an equal. Uncle Pete had been a model uncle, a man whom I always hoped to emulate. At Dartmouth in the 1920's Pete had personified the dashing exuberance of F. Scott Fitzgerald. Editor of the school newspaper, captain of Dartmouth's tennis team (and nationally seeded in doubles play), Pete had cut a romantic swath in his youth. Whatever spare time he had at college he spent bootlegging alcohol across the Canadian border. When he announced his engagement in 1924, a Bristol resident recalls that "You could open your window and hear the slow cracking of female hearts all over town."

As I grew up Pete, more than any other relative, sought me out to talk about politics, baseball, and women. His mind was encyclopedic and could dredge up facts which only children usually knew and considered important. Not only did my uncle know who made the only unassisted triple play in major league baseball (Bill Wambganss) but also the names of Wambganss's three victims.

I had only spoken to Pete over the phone during the last year and, while knowing that he was ill, I had not been told that he was dying from cancer. Now, sitting alone in Apley Court and rereading my aunt's letter I thought of my summer vacations in Bristol twenty years ago and my dreams of growing up like Uncle Pete. Now, in a strange twist, I was resembling him more than I wanted to.

Pete's death knocked a prop from under me. In my mind he had been somebody I could always turn to; I had planned to visit him during Easter. But now I was wondering whether cancer ran—or perhaps galloped uncontrollably—through the Howe family.

Up to a year ago, only Uncle Arthur. But my operation had been in August and since then a cousin, the broadcaster Quincy Howe, had died of cancer. And now, Uncle Pete.

"Does anybody else have it?" I wondered. And, once again, my frustration and anger arose at being helpless to control the uncontrollable. I flopped on the sofa, staring aimlessly at the ceiling.

To counteract my passivity I started to clean the room. The Seconal had made me too groggy to study but I was determined to do something worthwhile. A few wine and beer bottles lay by my desk along with a large stack of *Globe*s and assorted papers. I chucked the papers into the fireplace, thinking of the fire I'd have that evening. At three o'clock the pipes clanged once more. Grateful for an excuse to get outside, I pulled my coat on and departed.

A weak golden sun was setting upon Littauer as I wandered through Harvard Square and up Massachusetts Avenue towards Somerville. A solitary musician, apparently oblivious of the snow and cold, was stretched out snoring on a stone bench in Cambridge Commons. A few pigeons stalked uncertainly around him. A few months earlier, Baruch and I had wrestled for two hours in the early morning under the statue of Sir Thomas Dudley and then around the seesaws and swings. I remembered how ebullient and relaxed I had been arriving home at four in the morning. Now I felt tense and uncertain.

Cambridge symbols comforted me with their familiarity—the humming wires of the antiquated MBTA system; faded political prophecies that "NLF Will Win;" students nonchalantly carrying squash rackets; and old frame houses with their innumerable potted plants filling the windows. At the corner of Mass Ave and California Street, a bulldozer rested in a small pool of water. A middle-aged man with a newspaper tucked under his arm looked puzzled, as if he couldn't recollect what had once stood on that corner.

A cold rain began falling and I suddenly realized how exhausted I was. When I reached Porter Square, I turned for home. In a nearby yard a large white poodle stood on a lawn chaise longue, looking somewhat absently at the snow.

Passing by Oxford Street I gazed at the apartment where I had lived with Sarah, a Tufts university coed. In a short spasm of self-pity I wondered how different my life would now be if she and I hadn't broken apart. As much as I wanted to meet and understand my limits, I realized increasingly that I wanted a woman friend in whom I could confide completely.

Shivering from the walk, I sat in front of my fire, munched on a bacon and hamburger sandwich, and listened to records by Emmylou Harris and Linda Ronstadt. Once I had disdained such songs as "Bye Bye Love" and "Heart Like A Wheel" as vacuous emotings. But now I appreciated their releasing some of the anger and sadness within me.

The pipes began hammering once more. At eleven

o'clock, I limped wearily over to the phone and called the Buildings and Grounds department. I asked if they could lessen the noise, at least for this evening.

"Oh, yeah? And I've heard about you," answered a gruff-speaking maintenance man. "So how come we get more complaints from you than anybody else?"

I explained that I was taking medication at Stillman that tended to keep me awake.

"Hey, my heart bleeds for ya. Ya gonna tell me ya got cancer or sumpin'?"

I was too tired to play polite games. "Yes, I do have cancer," I replied. "And I've got to get enough sleep so I can keep taking the medication."

"No kiddin'?" The man from B and G thought for a moment and then asked, "Gee, what's it like?"

I shook my head in disbelief. "Who is this turkey?" I asked myself. Then, "Aw, you wouldn't believe it if I told you," I suggested.

Like many other people, the B and G man began to recount the cancer history of some friend or relative. Finishing his story he asked, "So has anything really strange happened to you like, you know, losing all your hair?"

To satisfy his ghoulishness, I replied, "Not only baldness. You can lose twenty, thirty, fifty pounds, be tired all day . . . and, of course, there's vomiting, a lot of diarrhea, possible genetic change, and heart damage." Pausing for effect I concluded, "And there's naturally the sexual problems—sterility and possible impotence."

He gave a low, wondering whistle. He finally responded, "No shit." Now he was in my corner. "Look, I don't think we can do much tonight but we'll try our best and, uh, I really hope everything turns out okay."

At one o'clock I collapsed into a fitful sleep. Two hours later I sprang up, suddenly awake and with a single, very clear thought. "I'm gonna die. I've got cancer. But I don't know when. An hour. A day. Ten years." I just knew that the cancer was still lurking inside me and that both its existence and timing were uncontrollable.

I swung my legs from the bed and tried to stand up, but fell onto the floor. Slowly I rose and, not wanting to turn on a light, fumbled along the wall. In the bathroom I vomited the hamburger-bacon sandwich. I was physically wrung out but totally alert.

I squirreled into the couch and stared impassively at the television. By two o'clock, only an evangelistic talk-and-music show and the movie "Dr. Strangelove" were still on. Without trying to follow the story, I watched the flickering screen as atom bombs blew up the world and the sound-track played "We'll Meet Again." When the national anthem began, I turned the set off and tried to sleep.

But the pipes kept clanging and early morning light soon filtered into the room. I started sobbing involuntarily from the exhaustion. Once more I got out of bed, swaying erratically, trying to reach the sofa. The unsettling combination of physical nervousness and mental exhaustion was rapidly overwhelming me.

Realizing that I should not have gone walking earlier, I concluded that I must return to Stillman. Could I get there by myself? It was six thirty A.M. I decided not to wake Debby or the other tutors. As I tied my running shoes I wondered if I could cross the street.

Fortunately, the cold morning air partially revived me. I stumbled across Holyoke Street and, holding upon the building for support, edged down the driveway to the emergency room. The usual five-minute trip seemed to last forever.

A middle-aged attendant reluctantly put down her copy of *Shogun* and, after completing the orange admittance form, told me to sit in the waiting room for a nurse. Bent over and breathing heavily, I prayed that the nurse hurry up. It was five minutes after seven.

Whenever I looked up, other waiting paitents were staring at me. Once a girl, who had been holding hands with her boyfriend, asked if I needed help. "No thanks," I replied.

An hour later the attendant reading *Shogun* finished

work. As she walked out she noticed me, hurried back be-
hind her desk, and spoke into the intercom. When a nurse
came to talk with me, she expressed some uncertainty that
Stillman should admit me.

I was beyond arguing. Quietly but firmly I said, "I'm not
leaving. Go and phone Conant." When she came back, she
accompanied me without comment to the fifth floor.

The next two days I spent in bed. Unable to sleep I
stared at the ceiling, not raising the shades to look outside
or let in any sunlight. Every evening I received increasing
dosages of such hypnotic drugs as chloral hydrate. Occa-
sionally I heard footsteps and whispers from the hallway.
Except for an infrequent nurse or doctor I didn't see any-
one. With each additional hour that I was awake I grew
increasingly angry and tense. The loss of sleep was self-
perpetuating.

On Tuesday afternoon, explaining that the change
would do me good, I obtained permission to go outside. I
had planned to wear my wig since I was going to the Har-
vard Coop. But the wind was too strong. Accordingly I en-
tertained myself with visions of my wig bounding across
Harvard Square while I plaintively cried, "Stop that wig."

When I sat down at my desk in Apley, I decided to
proofread the eighty new pages of my dissertation. The
thesis would remind me of the progress I had made despite
cancer and chemo. The thesis might also lessen my worries
about pain and sleeplessness.

The thesis wasn't on the desk so I searched through
each of the four drawers. It wasn't there. I looked behind
and under the desk and then in my bedroom. Even this
little activity made me tired. "Where," I wondered, "is that
damn thesis?"

With a crackling chill I thought of the papers that I had
cleaned up and then burned two nights previous. Before
rushing over for chemo to Stillman I had hurriedly placed
the thesis on top of the papers.

Moments arise which one instinctively understands are

turning points. As I gazed at the fireplace I realized that I had no chance of completing my dissertation this school year and that all my work toward that goal had been in vain. I could think only of the wasted effort. Other moments of despondency had arisen during the previous six months but I considered them temporary and overshadowed by the more important goal of completing the thesis. But now that was gone.

Back at Stillman I was angry and self-occupied as I paced my room. I couldn't stop walking and my left fist spasmodically crunched a rolled-up paperback. As nurses marched in with food, water pitchers, newspapers, and cookies I angrily shook my head. I didn't know what was happening but I couldn't bother myself with such trivia.

I stared outside at students scurrying through the snow, casually lofting snowballs on their way to friends and dinner. I muttered out loud, "Why me?" For the first time I decided that life was unfair.

I slammed my fist against the bathroom door. The pain crashed up my arm and I gave a muffled scream. I rested my head against the door and started sobbing. Everything that the doctors and I had done seemed unable to stop this cancer. We were all playing charades; I was going to die.

The optimism and pride of the last month now appeared as a cruel deception, something akin to placing a band-aid over a festering sore. After Cooperstown I had expected—expected, not merely hoped—to conquer cancer.

Now death appeared obvious, truly frightening. I would leave my friends who had helped me and who, without complaining, suffered with me. Death loomed as a bottomless black void, like the unexplored caves I entered in my youth when egged on by my friends. But this time nobody was going with me and there was no return. Donne's belief that death was only a short bridge could no longer comfort me. "Holy Jesus," I moaned. "I can't take this. The cancer's still there and I can't kill it."

The parents of a patient across the hall looked in to see what was wrong. Tears were streaming from my eyes. Never had I felt so lonely, so tired, so afraid. I sobbed, "No, please," and bent over to splash water on my face. I shut the door and slumped over the side of the bed.

Apparently somebody had alerted Conant. He took one look and sat down next to me. I reconstructed the last few hours, explained how I felt, and then asked, "What can I do?"

Part of Loring's effectiveness resulted from a low-key manner of listening and then suggesting, rather than pre-scribing. Since I always wanted to exert some control over my situation, I responded much more favorably to sugges-tion than to command. However falsely, it gave me the illusion of choice.

Conant didn't suggest anything right away but over the intercom ordered ten units of I.M. (intramuscular) Valium, then said that he wanted to check into something and would consult with me in the morning. After joking once more about Vinia's medical qualifications, he left. He had stayed only a few minutes and, while he had prescribed no cure, I felt immeasurably relieved.

A few hours after the Valium injection I received an-other hypnotic drug. "What if this one doesn't work?" I asked the nurse. "I guess nothing," she replied. "You've gone through all the drugs we're allowed to carry." Once more I lay still in the bed, for nine hours, wrestling with the dark while hoping against any reasonable assumption that I would sleep.

The next morning Conant bent over and studied my pained, twisted face. I had spent another night without sleep. I weakly suggested that the chemo was responsible for my problems.

"Herb, let's face the obvious." Loring's tone indicated a hesitancy to proceed. "I don't think that the primary prob-lem is physical. There's a doctor, a psychiatrist, at Massa-chusetts General who has helped a number of chemo patients. I'd like you to meet him." Loring studied me for a moment. "I hope you're not bothered by what I'm saying."

A year earlier I had silently scoffed at friends who visited psychiatrists. One should be able to work out one's own problems, I assumed. Now, after suffering near physical and mental breakdowns, I would be foolish to reject Loring's offer. I had reached the same conclusion as Loring, but hesitated to suggest it. Therefore I appreciated Conant's initiative.

Dr. Dwyer was an elderly man with glasses, white hair, and an encouraging smile. He patiently listened as I reviewed my last six months and my apprehensions about chemo's side effects and questionable effectiveness. Dwyer encouraged my growing sports schedule as a release from the uncontrollable aspects of my daily life. "Every cancer patient has to get beyond himself," Dwyer suggested. "All of us eventually surrender to the laws of gravity. But the essence of life is to resist as long as possible."

With the next session drawing nearer, both my friends and I concluded that I must have hit bottom with the last chemo; continued treatments were not only necessary but would be less painful. I grew in confidence daily. On the day before my next chemo I told Debby and Jane, "I think I'll lick it this time."

# Five

THE ROOM was absolutely quiet. Except for a sliver of light coming from under the bathroom door, I was surrounded by darkness. For seven hours after chemo I had travelled from bed to bathroom, vomiting, suffering occasional diarrhea along the way. At one o'clock, totally exhausted, I fell asleep. Now, an hour later, I was wide awake. Lying still, I wondered what had woken me.

Suddenly my body jerked and I started gagging. Sliding out of bed, I frantically tried to plant my feet on the foor. My legs collapsed from under me. I pitched forward against the closet. My head struck the oaken door and I lay motionless for several minutes. As I rose to a half-standing position, I clutched the wall for support and inched toward the bathroom. When I knelt over the toilet, my stomach muscles convulsed in a series of dry heaves. Pain twisted through my stomach and I started coughing uncontrollably.

After twenty minutes I leaned against the bathtub and gazed impassively at the green tiled wall. I thought of the last six months of first radiation and then chemo, and how each chemo session had weakened my resolve. In November and December, when I was still healthy, I had mustered enough courage to endure the treatments. Now, by January, chemo had worn me down. No matter how stoically I tolerated a chemo session, I would have to return three weeks later for another one. Faced with a possibly indefinite future of chemo, my courage rapidly diminished.

Over the last few weeks I pondered how chemo was ruining my life. By late fall I no longer considered myself a Harvard graduate student researching and teaching international affairs. I was a cancer patient, totally dependent upon forces which I could neither understand nor influence. I thought of Apley's clanging pipes, my sleeping pills, the chemo, and the inadequate insurance. "It's not that life is so unfair," I concluded, "but that it's so uncontrollable."

As I sat on the cold floor and stared at the green wall, I remembered that I was to have chemo later that day. I slumped forward, my head against my knees, and started sobbing. I knew that I could not continue.

Nurse's heels clacked down the hall. My bedroom door slid open and Laurie stepped in. A highly competent nurse, Laurie had quickly become a close personal friend. She was in her late twenties, physically attractive, and always warm toward others. During a recent lunch she had told me that "I get so much out of nursing. After college I knew that my social life would have to take a back seat."

Now squatting next to me, she took my hand and asked what was wrong. I shook my head. I wasn't going to complain. Tears kept streaming down my cheeks. She started to pull me up. I started sobbing again as she helped me into bed.

Tugging the blankets up to my shoulders Laurie looked compassionately at me. "Tell me what's bothering you," she requested. "It won't help either of us if you keep it locked up inside."

I gazed at the ceiling and thought of two more years of increasing pain and passivity. I turned to Laurie and sobbed, "This shit is killing me. I'm sorry, but this chemo's pure hell and I can't handle it. The chills, the vomiting, the diarrhea. God, I feel so helpless."

As Laurie sat on my bed she stroked my forehead and smiled. Physical touching often gave me a better cue about a person's feelings than any truckload of well-meant words. "Get a good night's rest," she said. "You'll feel differently tomorrow."

Shaking my head I persisted. "No, it's too much. I'm gonna quit the chemo."

Laurie looked at me for a long time, finally asking, "Have you told this to Conant?"

I would tell him that morning, I said. I squeezed Laurie's hands and looked gratefully at her. Our brief talk had drained off much of my tension. "Thanks, Laurie." She smiled softly and sat next to me until I drifted asleep.

A few hours later something seemed to be pinching my toes. I opened one eye reluctantly and focused upon Conant and a medical student peering at me from the foot of the bed. The bedside clock read a little after seven. Waiting for the inevitable question, I watched Conant pull out my chart, click his ballpoint pen, and study me.

"How do you feel this morning?"

I remember thinking that this was the moment of decision; after this, there would be no turning back. I knew that I would be disappointing Conant. He once had told me, "The worst aspect of being a doctor is giving painful medication, especially to a patient you like and respect." Perhaps he might consider his efforts wasted. But, at the same time, I felt some pride that I was now controlling my life.

"I'm stopping the chemo."

Conant arched his eyebrows and hesitated. "Today's treatment, you mean?"

I sighed and shook my head. I explained why I was quitting and that I strongly appreciated his concern and patience. The medical student shifted nervously as Conant lowered his head in thought.

"You know what you're doing?"

"Yes."

"You understand the possible implications if you stop the chemo?"

I silently recalled Grey turning away from his office window and bluntly stating to me, "You can live three hundred days or thirteen thousand days. It's your choice."

"Yes, I've thought about it." The medical student glanced quickly at both of us and left.

For the next ten minutes Conant exercised his quiet persuasiveness and impressed upon me the need to continue treatments. Respectfully agreeing about the possible need, I reiterated that I had reached my limit. "I wish I were a better person so that I could continue. But if I've only got a couple of months left anyway, I've got to make the most of them." I glanced at a greeting card sent by a former girlfriend. It showed a forlorn medieval knight clutching his jaw while the inscription read "For there was never yet a philosopher that could endure the toothache patiently." Turning to Conant I concluded, "If I am dying, I want to do it my own way."

Conant nodded and wrote a lengthy note on my chart before talking to me. "I respect you," he began "and so I'll respect your decision. But, since we're more than halfway finished with a six month's protocol, I'll ask one condition. Promise me that you'll think seriously about your decision and, after a couple of days, come by to discuss it with me and Dr. Grey. You owe that much to us and yourself."

As Conant pocketed his pen, he paused. Then, leaning down he touched my shoulder and said, "You're a very human person in a very difficult position. But you've got more friends than you'll ever know and we want you to live." Unable to say anything, I simply nodded. A nurse entered with my breakfast and Conant left.

Snow was quietly falling as I left Stillman and walked down to the Charles, past the Fly Club, Professor Fairbank's yellow frame house, and through the courtyard of Kirkland House. It was the same route that Danny and I had run a month previous.

I crossed Memorial Drive and glanced at the Charles's stately sycamores. Their branches, bare of any leaves, stood motionless. The gray skies promised several more days of stormy weather. As I walked along the path paralleling the river, I pictured Grey turning to me and saying, "It's your choice."

"Choice?" How much easier that word had sounded those few weeks earlier. Now the pain, the exhaustion, the fear, and the anger of being kept from immediate goals precluded any choice in the matter. Lacking the courage to face chemo, I was permitting any remaining cancer to destroy me. Stunned that I had lost my battle, I walked until late afternoon.

As the snow continued to fall I met Jon for dinner at a Chinese restaurant. Jon and I had been only moderate friends until he learned that I had cancer. Immediately he and Norah rallied around me, coupling their strong caring with an irreverent humor. They had more than compensated for a few formerly close friends leaving me upon hearing about my cancer.

I watched Jon ease his six-foot, four-inch body onto the small wicker chair. His black beard and piercing, almost mystical, eyes suggested a Hollywood version of an Old Testament prophet. Jon leaned back and listened silently as I bitterly described the past two days and my anger at my limitations.

"And you think you've failed, Herb?"

"Of course. The protocol has a minimum run of six months but I've quit after two." I slowly shook my head. "That certainly sounds like failure to me."

"You're wrong."

Jon drew in a deep breath and leaned towards me. "Hey, I know what you're going through. Your whole damn life has flipped out of control. You've had your hair fall out, you haven't been laid, you've been tired most of the time, and you're in trouble with your thesis. But you've kept your spirits up, haven't asked for pity, and sure played sports harder than ever. And, you did all that while doing your thesis and the teaching. So, now you're kvetching?" He grinned broadly, "Hey, gimme a break, okay?"

As we ate dinner Jon said that I had been going the limit against absurd odds. He compared me to an amateur runner who suddenly has to compete against an Olympic champion. "Okay, so you lose the race. But if you gave it your real best, you didn't lose a thing. And with you, the point is that you've kept going back to chemo, despite all the shit it caused. It's as if you were trying to defy fate, to see your limits."

Jon looked intently at me and shook his head. "To all of us you may have lost an unwinnable war, but you've been winning an even more impressive battle. And we want to see you keep winning."

I nodded gratefully and considered the sports analogy. Conant and I had recently discussed my growing athletic schedule. During an increasingly bleak winter, athletics had drained off some of my tension and made me feel less dependent upon medical technology. A recent medical article had correlated high levels of stress with cancer and had suggested that sports, through a complex chemical sequence, could reduce the size of certain tumors. I looked out the restaurant's window at the cold dark night. "Perhaps it's quackery," I reflected, "but it does offer hope."

On our way back to Apley we paused outside the Indoor Athletic Building. We stood perfectly still, watching the snow drift through pools of yellow streetlight. Finally, Jon motioned towards the gym. "Sports have helped you so far. But you've had a really rough two days, so don't do anything crazy now. Stay away from here."

I resented Jon's well-meant advice. After admitting defeat from chemo, I didn't want any more reminders of my limitations. "Maybe I'll work out tomorrow," I looked at Jon. "Just to see how I feel."

Jon stared unbelievingly at me. Then, raising his mittened hands to beseech some heavenly divinities he pleaded, "Keep this turkey away from his running shoes, okay?" After promising to play squash with me in a week, Jon bid goodby and trudged up a snow-filled Holyoke Street.

One of the reasons I enjoyed sports at Harvard was their total lack of pretense. I didn't have to wear a wig or bury myself in bulky clothes to disguise any weight loss. And locker room conversations steered clear of Hobbes's purported liberalism or Wilson's sociobiology while enthusiastically examining the relative merits of Ted Williams and Fred Lynn or how to improve one's crawl stroke.

When I entered the locker room on Wednesday morning, an emeritus physics professor was talking to Professor Williams. Williams was smiling and nodding appreciatively as the older professor held forth on his first and only run in the 1928 Boston marathon. As I walked into the showers, Williams turned his head and smiled a quick recognition.

The pool, which has since been supplanted by a Roman lake in the new Dillon Center, was once considered one of America's premier pools. John Kennedy swam backstroke for Harvard before the war, and a plaque and photo commemorate this fact. In the photo, the young Kennedy is slightly bent over in a distinctly nonprofessional diving stance.

In the bleachers hang photos of past varsity swimming teams. For the year 1932, my father is standing determinedly, with arms folded across his chest, trying to invoke absent muscles to rise. As I entered the pool I smiled at my father's photo. I thought of the daily practices which had tested his ability and desire. Another generation of Howes swimming at Harvard. It was a source of strength and continuity.

The large, chlorine-green pool was full of swimmers churning laps before lunch or the next class. I felt dizzy as I stepped between the red and blue kickboards. Hopefully, the swimming would take my mind off any weakness while possibly making me stronger. Diving in, I broke the surface half a lane down.

"Better take it easy, no sense in spurting today," I cautioned myself. I commenced an easy crawl at about half speed, noticed the turn markers twelve feet below me, spun into a quick flip turn and pushed off quickly from the pool's end. My timing on the turn had been excellent. I smiled broadly (usually a most unnatural act when your face is underwater) and stepped up the pace. At the end of the length I flipped again, timed my pushoff correctly, and glided a good fifteen feet before surfacing.

Florence Chadwick, the world's most famous marathon swimmer, once explained her long training sessions by noting, "Life in the water is less complicated." The morning's swim was recharging me. I thought back to my last chemo sessions. Yesterday's confrontation with Conant no longer seemed important. My pride in pulling against the water and rolling into a flip turn washed away any notions of defeat, dejection, and death. As my arms jerked free of the water, poised themselves above my head, and then pierced the surface and pulled back, various muscles strained against the tension. I felt exhilarated.

On the fourth lap I shifted into my racing pace, which sacrifices any remaining aesthetics for increased speed. My legs pumped furiously while my arms discarded a once regulated rhythm for a sheer paroxysm of getting into and through the water as rapidly as possible.

I had sprinted about fifteen feet. Suddenly all sensation drained from my legs. My head felt faint, almost limp. I had lost most of my strength. Terrified, I strove to leave the pool. I tried sprinting. My arms couldn't leave the water. With my legs motionless I drifted into a vertical, near helpless position. I remember thinking, "I've got cancer but I'm gonna die drowning in a swimming pool."

I looked around. Other swimmers pounded on, oblivious of my situation; the lifeguard had contentedly curled up with a textbook. My head tilted back. "Can't swallow water," I told myself. But then I started coughing, as water lapped into my mouth. By reflex I finally started treading water and, as a bit of energy returned, I dogpaddled over to the pool's steps. I wound my arms around the railing. With amazement I realized that I was too weak to leave the pool. After several minutes I caught my breath, pulled myself out, and flopped onto a nearby wooden bench. With my head between my legs, I pondered what had happened. Never before had physical activity left me so vulnerable. Bending over me, a member of Dudley's Senior Common Room asked if I was all right. "I'm fine," I told him.

As I lingered under a hot shower, my fear of having almost drowned gave way to pride. I had pushed myself beyond any reasonable expectation. Twenty-four hours earlier, I had been lying helpless and defeated in Harvard's infirmary. Now, I had swum myself to near exhaustion while still having the power to recover from a possibly fatal situation. Pride was replacing pity and fear. As I strolled home, a cold northeast wind blasted against my face. I felt alive.

By late afternoon, I had completed my African politics tutorial, so I relaxed with a mug of hot chocolate. Tilting back in my captain's chair, I propped my feet on the windowsill and gazed out upon Holyoke Street. Students bent against the bitter wind. Old newspapers dipped, soared, and scurried along the pavement.

I sipped the cocoa. The debate between myself and the doctors was no longer about chemotherapy but about life and death, which once would have made the choice quite easy. I thought back to Claudia and our last night together. I had watched her face glow with excitement as she described the pride she took from constantly setting new goals. Suddenly she had pointed at the Picasso print of two hands clasping orange and red flowers. "We're here on earth only once," she exclaimed, "so we've got to grab life and squeeze it for all its worth." I thought about Claudia's optimistic, peppery view of life. I had to believe in my ability to outlast and conquer obstacles.

Shortly before my operation I had called Cooperstown to chat. Charlie innocently asked if I wanted to compete with him, Smoky, and Stephanie in a canoe race on Memorial Day. "Sure," I replied. A few days before leaving Cambridge I called Lin to tell her when my bus would arrive in Albany. "What's this about a canoe race?" I asked her.

"Charlie didn't tell you about it?"

"No," I replied, "not really."

"Dearest brother," she asked, "how much canoeing have you done?"

I recalled a tedious afternoon when I was ten years old at a church camp. "I got bored after ten minutes of paddling and quit."

My sister tried to control her laughter. "Well," she finally began, "the competitors come from all over the U.S., Canada, and other countries." She paused, obviously relishing her next statement. "It's seventy-two miles long and is the longest single-day canoe race in the world. Oh, and it's also the world's championship."

Charlie and I practiced for a few hours on the day before the race. At the dinner table Willie, my seven–year–old nephew, scoffed. "Are you really gonna race tomorrow? Boy, are you crazy." I made a mental note about a child's natural wisdom.

As the first rays of sun spilled over Cooperstown, Lin knocked hesitantly at my door. "I'm already dressed," I grumbled morosely. "I couldn't sleep at all and I don't think I want to do this race."

From an adjoining room Smoky mumbled, "I don't think any of us got much sleep. But we're here and we're gonna do it." Confronted with such familial assumptions I had no choice.

Through the rising mist Charlie and I and Smoky and Stephanie paddled towards the starting line of one hundred and fifty canoes. My back muscles started protesting. I searched for fellow sufferers. With a multicolored headband, streaks of black pigment under his eyes, and a nose completely whitened with suntan lotion, the canoeist next to us resembled a modern day Indian.

"Have you canoed much before?" I inquired.

He perused our clunker of a canoe and grinned. "Sure

have," he finally replied. "I've done this race since it opened thirteen years ago. Me and my buddy spend our weekends driving to different races. Drove down from Montreal for this one." He squinted at the early morning sun and, with a straight face, said "I hope you make it before nightfall." I laughed uneasily. So much for commiseration.

For several hours we paddled furiously; pain tugged at my unprepared muscles. Thirty-five miles later we spotted Lin and the children waving from under an old stone bridge. We jumped ashore and wolfed down orange juice and candy bars. "Why don't you rest?" asked Lin. Charlie looked inquiringly at me. I surprised myself by answering, "No. We're going to finish the race the best we can." Charlie shrugged and we pushed off.

During the remaining hours we ran with our canoe over two portages, stroked through the sargasso Goodyear lake, and shot a couple of white water areas. The sun disappeared; rain soaked us for the next twenty-five miles. By five o'clock my only interest was sighting canoes ahead of us and then paddling furiously to overtake them. Once I had told myself that we would finish the race, any pain seemed almost incidental.

We pulled across the Bainbridge finishline at seven in the evening. It was twelve hours since we had started from Cooperstown; the winners had arrived four hours earlier. Meeting up with Smoky and Stephanie at the awards stand, we sat around eating fried chicken and congratulating each other on the day's accomplishment.

Stephanie had draped herself in bulky woolen sweaters in a losing effort to stop shivering. But her enthusiasm was equally uncontrollable. She brushed back her wet hair and started laughing. "I can't believe it! If you'd told me in January that we could do this race—wow, I'd have said you were crazy. Look at us, will ya? We did something we thought was impossible."

Still shaking, Stephanie hugged me. "And you, Herb. You were bitching this morning about never reaching

Bainbridge. But, you did it! So wipe that smile off your face, you crazy lunk." I nodded and grinned even more widely. I had been amazed by my determination. Three months after the race, I was operated on for cancer.

Now, on a January night I sat alone, thinking of chemotherapy and balancing its pain with the alternative of possible death. I wondered if I could ever again subject myself to the three drugs. With the loss of my thesis I could make no substantial academic progress within the next three weeks. I required a short-term challenge. Sports could offer an emotional release and the chance of rapid progress. I had to believe that I could overcome obstacles. I remembered how proud I had been after Cooperstown. Perhaps sports could build up my self-confidence. Lifting the receiver off its hook, I quickly fell asleep.

After breakfast I stopped off at Conant's office. Conant told me that Grey was considering an unusual regimen: a single day treatment every three weeks. "We are worried about it," Conant emphasized, "because we've never tried it before. Three drugs on the same day; they'll present a strong trauma to your system."

He paused and leaned back in his chair. "Have you decided whether you'll continue the chemo?" As I studied my duffel bag I shook my head. "Nope. But, I'll let you and Grey know fairly soon."

"I hope so," Conant replied. "It may be the only way out."

While changing into my running shoes I wondered how far I could run. A few desultory snowflakes hung in the air as I entered Harvard Yard. I half-ran, half-slipped across the pavement's ice. A becoming snowy wig topped John Harvard's statue. As I reached the Science Center I picked up my pace and ran along Oxford Street: Agassiz, Perkins, the law school, and Lesley College. My breathing sounded easy and controlled. A sensual pleasure warmed me as my legs reached for the pavement. I felt in control of myself.

Past the old yellow frame house that had housed Ryan

O'Neal and Ali McGraw in *Love Story*. At the end of Oxford Street I scampered over an old railroad bridge and thought back to the weightroom in early October. I had been straining under a 150-pound lift when a heavyset man with closely cropped hair entered. Vivaldi's "Gloria" blasted from his tape recorder. He asked if I would adjust a bar for two hundred pounds. "Why can't he do it himself?" was my first thought. Then I looked closely at him. His eyes were fixed straight ahead. A white cane stuck out from under his down jacket.

During the next few months I marvelled at the man's equability and quiet determination. He could press one hundred pounds more than I had ever attempted. One afternoon he had told me that he had started lifting weights after becoming blind: "I needed something to make me feel less handicapped." When not weightlifting, he pursued his doctoral studies in Harvard's physics department.

As I ran down Beacon Street and over to Lechmere, I pictured his look of quiet determination as he strained to heave the weights above his head. I picked up my pace. My shoes squished as they struck the pavement. Outside a Red Cross center, two old women were leaning on each other as they maneuvered up the icy path.

I turned the corner at Oxford, ran across the bridge again, and thought of my sixty-five-year-old father. For the last nine years he has quietly conspired against the natural laws of aging. He belongs to a largely unheralded yet eminently praiseworthy group called the A.A.U. Master Swimmers.

At 5 A.M., six days a week, rain, sun, or sleet, he bicycles to the local swimming pool. Swimmers, pre-teen to senior citizens, splash furiously up and down the pool. By 7:30 he has sprinted two miles.

After his morning swim, he pedals into the University of Wisconsin, where he has taught classics for thirty years. Following some teaching and research, he strolls to a nearby pool where he swims a third mile. He won two letters in swimming at Harvard but stopped serious swim-

ming upon graduation. In 1950, after the birth of this third
and last child, he turned again to the pool. He swam two
hundred miles that year. In 1976 he stroked 810 miles, or
the distance from New York to Chicago. For his efforts he
has won four national titles in his age group and es-
tablished two national records.

I had always expressed bemusement at my athletic fa-
ther clumping down the stairs shortly after I had climbed
them to go to sleep. How could any intelligent adult spend
so much time performing such a seemingly monotonous
activity as swimming up and down a swimming pool? One
night I asked him what drove master swimmers to practice
three hours a day.

After joking that swimming is the one sport which you
can enjoy lying down, my father offered that "once in a
while the sheer esthetic delight of shooting an arm out, rid-
ing onto it as the shoulder dips, catching, hooking, and
thrusting back is just an ecstasy of physical pleasure—to
hell with beating people." He thought for a moment. "Com-
petition exists, but it is largely against oneself. I think the
older we've become, the less we care about beating other
people."

He told me of Nellie Brown, who lives in Virginia.
Stricken with polio, Nellie started swimming for therapy
over forty years ago. Several years ago she realized that
master swimming could increase her incentive to over-
come a medical history of polio, glaucoma, cataracts, and a
broken back. Joining the Washington D.C. Masters at age
eighty, she quickly became a national champion. Four
years later she was America's oldest swimming champion.

My father concluded that swimming proves aging is not
an inexorable process. Unlike top-flight collegiate swim-
mers who peaked in their twenties, "We've just enjoyed
getting better as time tries to pass us by. Three years ago,
my time for the 1650 was 27:07; last spring, 24:17. We're
all in a losing war with time, but I've enjoyed winning some
of the skirmishes."

I was panting hard as I reached the Science Center. "If

that blind weightlifter, my father, and Nellie Brown can do
so well, then I sure as hell have no excuses." Throwing my
head back I sprinted across the Yard. I disregarded every-
thing except an imaginary finish line outside of Words-
worth House. I strained with my chest, snapped the imagi-
nary tape, tried to stop, and banged against Anderson gate.
I had run six miles. In three weeks, I decided, I would run
eight miles daily. I jogged to the I.A.B., changed, and then
plunged into the pool. Up, then back; flip, stroke, and pull.
Four times as many laps as the day before.

But the fears that had caused my breakdown and which
had been intensified by my recent chemo decision soon re-
turned. After having a late dinner with Debby and Brian, I
walked back alone to Apley. Suddenly I felt alone and vul-
nerable. "It's possible that I'll die tonight but I can't do any-
thing to stop it." I started sobbing in the cold night air. My
nose started running and I cursed my helplessness. When
a friend shouted something from across the street, I waved
him off. No one was going to see me like this. The pipes
were already clanging as I entered my room. I swallowed
four Dalmanes and toppled into a fitful sleep.

The next day I felt hung over from the sleeping pills. I
taught tutorials until two o'clock, at which time I wrapped
my wrists, gathered my speedgloves, and jogged to the
I.A.B. The boxing room was empty except for four young
blacks practicing Tae Kwon Do. As I loosened up I mar-
velled at their flexible, nearly liquid movements. As they
combatted imaginary enemies, their legs and arms quickly
flicked out and then curled back effortlessly.

I grabbed two pulley weights, yanking them down to
my knees. The motion reminded me of canoeing and I
thought of the Memorial Day race. What better incentive
existed for improving myself daily than preparing to win
this year's race? My back muscles, and then the deltoids
and triceps, stretched with the increasing pressure. Pulling
the weights down to my ankles, I watched sweat drip off
the tip of my nose onto the shining floor.

During Christmas vacation in Cooperstown Lin had

asked me, "Is there anything worse than death?" I paused as her three children stormed through the living room on their way to a neighborhood snowball fight.

"Realizing that you've lived an unfulfilled life, I suppose. Time is precious and I think I've wasted a lot of it. I have to decide what I want and then pursue it as if there's no tomorrow. Then, when death comes, I'll be happy. I'll have done my best."

I stalked the swaying body bag, imagining it to be a large cancer cell. There are moments in life when the mind excuses itself and allows the body to take over. I remember nothing about the next twenty minutes. My self-absorption in pounding the bag was complete.

Eventually I noticed that the four blacks were standing around me. "Excuse me, sir." The Tae Kwon Do teacher stepped towards me. "We've been watching you box. You've got a nice reach and respectable power. And, you're left handed. We don't have much opportunity to practice against someone like you." He smiled at me. "Would you like to spar for a round?"

Blinking, I looked beyond him to his students. Although they were gazing impassively at me, I imagined they were thinking, "Teach sure gonna wipe this honky."

"Me box you?" I considered this absurd offer. Since Tae Kwon Do utilizes both feet and hands, any boxer faces a disadvantage. And, whereas I was a novice at boxing, my stock opponent had a black belt loosely wrapped around his white uniform.

"Sure, I'll do it." I bounced nervously up and down. "as long as you don't kick below the belt." The confident teacher smiled and bowed twice. "He's saying grace before dinner," I speculated.

Before I realized anything, his right leg rammed twice against my ribs. I quickly moved to my right. A painful left hook thudded against my ear. I jabbed futilely, threw three crosses which only encountered air, and received two jabs on my nose in return.

The disadvantage of orthodoxy is its predictability. After

a minute of observation, my boxing style is totally predictable. I soon realized that my opponent could anticipate every feint, jab, and clinch. So, disregarding scripture, I led with my left. Two left leads popped him and I quickly followed with a right hook to the ribs. His students doubled over in laughter. "Watch fo'm, look out fo'm, he's a big white hope." Their teacher backpedaled and studied his heavily breathing opponent who was sporting an immense grin of accomplishment. I had briefly taken control of a seemingly hopeless situation. The teacher tugged at his mouthpiece and lifted his hands to indicate the round's end.

"You're not very good yet. Too hesitant, too slow, too easy to counter." He smiled reassuringly and continued to appraise me. "But you think on your feet and you keep going. Would you like to go a round with each of my students?"

For the next half hour I enthusiastically puffed after elusive and well-conditioned martial arts students. Occasionally landing a blow, I was amazed at their quickness. At four o'clock I wearily stepped back and announced my surrender. "Shit, I can't take this no more."

The students laughed and approached me. My knees wobbled like wet spaghetti, my nose was bleeding, and my fists ached (not from landing many blows but from being clenched for the better half of an hour).

After we shook hands, I thanked them and headed for the door. As I pulled the doorknob I felt a hand on my back. Turning, I faced the teacher.

"Thanks very much," he said. "I didn't think you'd agree to it, and I sure didn't think that you'd last. You just hang in there and I think that's really fine." I nodded my appreciation, said I'd drop by again, and then walked slowly but happily to the showers.

In the locker room I paused to look at myself in the mirror. Chemo had robbed me of my hair and had given me a pale gaunt appearance. Sports, however, had forced my once flabby body to lose twenty pounds since August and to acquire new muscle. When I was younger, the value of sports had come from defeating other people and teams. As that ethic faded after grade school, so did my athletic activity. By seventh grade I had discarded my dreams of playing first base for the Milwaukee Braves. Despite earlier accomplishments, I never won a letter in high school. College, Peace Corps, and graduate school pigeon-holed my athletic enthusiasm to pick-up games and infrequent swimming or jogging.

Now sports were acquiring a new meaning. Instead of competing against other people I would be battling both myself and the effects of chemotherapy. To sustain myself through chemo I had to believe that neither my spirit nor my body were decaying. I thought of what my father, Nellie Brown, and the weightlifter had received from sports.

Writing about athletics, Michael Novak described winning as "a form of thumbing one's nose, for a moment, at the cancers and diseases that, in the end, strike us all down." I just had to win.

I wondered whether athletics would replace academics as my chief goal at Harvard. If I could run, canoe, swim, and box harder and longer than I had thought possible, could I complete my dissertation and chemotherapy? "What," I wondered, "are my real limitations?"

I dressed and quickly walked home. Picking up the phone I called Grey's office. I told him that I had talked to Dr. Conant that morning.

"I'd like to see you within the next few days to discuss the new protocol."

"Certainly." Grey thought for a moment. "Does this mean that you'll be continuing with chemotherapy?"

"Yes," I replied, "it does."

# Six

DURING THE NEXT FEW DAYS I realized that my decision was final, that I would complete the six months of chemotherapy.

I suffered no second doubts. I was pleased that my survival depended more upon my resources than upon medical science. All medical advances were worthless unless I could absorb the chemotherapy.

After seven months of flailing within the whirlwind of expert oncologists, surgeons, social workers, X-ray diagnosticians, unseen lab specialists, nurses, Dr. Conant, and the Boston hospital system I now faced cancer alone. Now, it was *my* struggle.

I shunted aside doubts about chemo's possible side effects. I knew that I would still grouse about taking chemo, as well as vomiting and having diarrhea, but that every three weeks I would find myself in Stillman.

I grabbed sports as eagerly as a schoolchild pulls on his first Little League jersey. Sports emphasized my disinclination to depend upon friends. Friends couldn't give me what I needed most: pride in myself, a sense of control, and a chance to test myself against an intimidating foe.

In the late summer and early fall I had hesitated to seek help because I had worried about appearing as a pitiable burden. Yet, prompted by genuine friendship or the guilt of the innocent, numerous friends volunteered their services. My closest friends bitterly attacked me for not accepting their offers. When I told Debby of my decision to walk, physically exhausted, to Stillman alone, she snapped "You're a big, fuckin' pain in the ass when it comes to needing people. We want to help but you refuse it. Just how do you think we feel?"

But their well-meaning aid, rides to hospitals, ice cream, greeting cards, and telephone calls underscored a dependence which I didn't want. And friendly assurances quickly lost their assuring quality. They became too expected and fixed, a never changing litany.

Work on my thesis became meaningless. Stunned by its loss, I knew that I needed immediate accomplishment. Yet completion and publication would require many months of devoted work.

Friends inquired whether philosophy served any use. "All those classes must have taught you something," Jon argued. But outside of Rousseau's *Second Discourse* and its arguments about human development, political theory was too abstract to grapple with a day-to-day situation. The present, as described by Robert Frost, was "Too much for the senses, too crowded, too confusing, too present to imagine."

Such friends as Jane and Debby asked if I knew what caused my cancer and if I felt anger at anybody because of it. But I never seriously speculated about the cause; too many possibilities existed and, furthermore, the knowledge would be useless. I needed to deal with the present, rather than bemoan the past. During my first night at Bristol I had bitterly wondered, "Why me?" wondering what I had done to deserve cancer. Now I simply shrugged and asked, "Why not me?"

I had briefly felt angry towards Dr. Dunn. Those four days I had spent at Baptist Hospital and Stillman wondering whether I had cancer still rankled. One evening I told Norah, "I'd rather have known my position than wonder about it."

"Maybe they think it's kinder not to tell."

"Kinder? Kinder for whom?" I retorted. "By not telling me, he's implying that I can't handle adversity. That's the type of kindness I can do without."

Hoping to dispel my resentment, I visited Dunn several days later. I left impressed by the difficulties a doctor has with possibly dying patients.

"I hadn't seen you ever before, not 'till you came into my Harvard office," Dunn began. "I guessed there was about a fifty percent chance that your lump was cancer. But I'll never mention cancer to a patient unless I'm sure he has it. An associate of mine once mentioned to a patient that he had a tumor. Well, the patient assumed that it was cancer and shot himself."

My lump had been difficult to diagnose. As I lay anaesthetized on a marble slab, Dunn opened my wrist. Along with two other doctors he examined the soft tissue tumor. It resembled a white grape.

"It's benign. That's for certain," offered one of the doctors as the other nodded concurrence. Dunn weighed in with a minority opinion. "It's fibrosarcoma and it's definitely malignant."

As I continued to lie unconscious the three doctors continued their debate.

"It is benign. It certainly doesn't look bad. And if we remove it, we might have to sever the entire tendon. His records show that he's just turned thirty-one and he looks athletic. Without the tendon he might lose the use of a finger."

"Either he loses the finger or he loses his life," countered Dunn.

Thirty minutes later Dunn won the debate. He removed the flexordigitorum muscle and tendon to the tip of the index finger. He then sutured the severed tendon onto the tendon of another finger. My middle finger retained about seventy percent of its previous strength and mobility.

Substantial uncertainty still remained about the identity of my tumor. The hospital pathologist provisionally diagnosed histiocytic fibrosarcoma, based on a frozen biopsy. "But we needed conclusive findings before telling you," Dunn recalls.

While I lay in Baptist and then Stillman, my tumor slides were flown across the country to such institutions as the Armed Forces Institute of Pathology in Washington, as well as being specially delivered by taxi to numerous Boston specialists.

By Friday most of the diagnoses came back: the patient has a serious form of histiocytic fibrosarcoma. At best he has a twenty percent survival chance.

"I knew that I'd have to tell you Saturday," said Dunn. "But sitting around the kitchen table with my wife on Friday night I had a terrible, lousy feeling. At the same time I had another really serious case, a fifteen-year-old boy. I knew that I had to tell both of you. But I sure couldn't get myself up for it. That's why I might have appeared somewhat fumbling when we talked the next morning."

As I left Dunn's office he asked if I had seen other doctors before coming to him about the bump. "Two or three," I said. Shaking his head in disbelief, Dunn complimented me on my persistence. "Your life was saved by your attention to it. Otherwise, you would've died by December."

Viewed from the outside, Harvard's Indoor Athletic Building appears strikingly handsome, with its towering red brick gently augmented with white trim. But inside, peeling paint competes successfully against numerous plastering attempts. And smells of sweat and liniment from forgotten struggles of forty years pervade the locker and weight rooms. But to me, the I.A.B. contrasted favorably to manicured and antiseptic hospital rooms.

Each day I climbed the three flights of stairs and entered the exercise rooms. I thought increasingly of the world's championship canoe race on Memorial Day in Cooperstown. The race gave me another explanation for my athletics.

As I started with fifty-pound lifts and jerks and curls, I

could feel tributaries of sweat trickle down and then collect under my arms, in the small of my back, and above my knees. Sweat became a sign of work, sacrifice, and determination.

As I jerked or pushed bars of over 160 pounds I smiled, realizing that such accomplishments would have seemed impossible, and somewhat foolish, only a few months before. While lifting, I thought about the race. Was Charlie in shape, how could we improve the canoe, and how quickly could we race in his heavy, eighty-pound canoe? Is there a maximum speed for the canoe, I wondered, or is our strength more important than the boat's design and weight? I looked at a row of stacked barbells. I had no chance to learn sophisticated strokes or how to "read" a river. I would be pitting my endurance against the endurance and skills of other racers.

After an hour of lifting I would sense the stretching of different tendons and nerves of my body. I felt better than ever before. Perhaps I needed a perfect body to balance against, and then improve, my imperfect resolve about chemo. I looked at myself in a nearby mirror. "It may be narcissism," I concluded, "but it's damn important for me right now."

The significance of sports was growing. One evening in late February I had sullenly moped home; Jon had trounced me in five straight squash games. My immediate anger was heightened by the knowledge that not so long ago I could defeat Jon. Yet now, falling behind after the first few points, I would give up, convinced that continued struggle was futile.

As I walked home I gradually realized that Jon (or Bob or Danny) was no longer my opponent. A squash match would be forgotten after several days. But perhaps I could learn something lasting. If I could rebound from a thirteen-to-two deficit or if I could run further two days after chemo than I ever thought possible, then perhaps I could snub my nose at chemo and its undeniable pain.

In its small way, athletic defeat approximated death. Both were inevitable and not necessarily painful. The more familiar defeat became, the less I might fear death. As I spent increasing hours in the I.A.B., Hemenway, and along the Charles I concluded that defeat could emerge as a natural and neutral occurrence. It could lose its sting if I competed as fiercely as possible against the stiffest possible odds.

On a sunny, Sunday February afternoon some fellow Dudley students and I grabbed a basketball and marched over to the I.A.B. to battle a pick-up team from Eliot House. But against a far superior team we soon fell behind. No matter how hard we tried, we could not penetrate their defense. They were taller, faster, and worked together much better as a team.

Then, as the enemy approached the twenty-one points necessary to win, our side suddenly caught fire. Larry Dwyer began setting picks for Bob Sullivan who popped in two rapid baskets from the baseline. Then I hit my first basket, a gorilla push from downtown. Amidst the frenzied squeak of sneakers we started laughing at the absurdity. We were playing far better than we actually were and nothing could go wrong.

Despite its lead, Eliot House began to fall apart. Worried glances quickly gave way to bitter accusations. Driving against a scowling, taller opponent, Kevin Dougherty grinned as he shifted the ball from one hand to the other in midair and dropped it through the hoop. We pressed uncompromisingly on defense. No longer did we care about winning. We were celebrating something else, perhaps our belief that we couldn't give in easily. Unrestrained and unthinking, we scampered about for the next ten minutes. Finally our opponents scored their last two points. We were exhausted but elated, while Eliot House appeared confused.

We were toweling ourselves off and pulling on running suits as two Eliot players wandered over. "You guys really caught fire," one of them said. "And we thought we had you. Just what the hell happened?" Shouts and admonitions drifted over from games in the other courts as Larry Dwyer grinned and shook his head. "Just one of those things, I guess."

We had lost, but our defeat seemed meaningless. For a few minutes we had thumbed our noses at the inevitable. For fifteen minutes we had played far better than we ever thought possible; we had not surrendered after our dismal beginning.

Every day, except during chemo, I tried to accomplish more than I had done the day or week before. In January I had averaged six-minute miles. In February I averaged four sub-six-minute miles as well as the usual swimming and squash. In March I averaged just slightly over five minutes per mile each day. In addition, I was playing squash and then baseball for Dudley's intramural teams.

Special moments emerged. During February and March I felt the sun warm my bald, sweating head as I ran across Dillon's playing fields. I would sprint towards the setting sun, running faster as the sun continued to set. One day in early March I ran to the Museum of Science and back (a distance of ten miles) and then impulsively ran another five miles to Allston. No amount of pain in my knees could lessen my satisfaction that day.

Friends began to worry more about my athletic pace than about the possibility of my dying from cancer. Arriving an hour late for dinner, I explained to Jane that I had played four matches of squash instead of two. I blinked as Jane angrily asked, "Do you have *any* idea of what you're doing to your body?" Sitting back she looked at me and shook her head. "If I was able," she noted, "I'd kick you in the seat of your pants and then, for good measure, do it again."

My scuba instructor, a man I admired, once took me aside and confided that "more people than you'd think know about your cancer. We're praying for your recovery,"

he said, "but now you're trying to complicate everything."
He looked sternly at me. "Herb," he asked, "do you have a
death wish?"

And even Jon, who had distinguished himself at Tufts
by playing four hours of basketball a day, yet still graduat-
ing *magna cum laude,* lambasted my sports. When he
heard that I had gone running and then had boxed a day
before chemo he likened me to a former baseball player—
"You're just like Babe Herman. Ain't got no sense, catching
flyballs with your head. But go ahead; you're sure not using
it for much else."

I heeded Loring the most. He knew me well, wanted
the best for me, and was a doctor. We discussed my grow-
ing athletic schedule whenever we met. On Wednesday in
early February Loring and I stood talking in the anteroom
of the Senior Common Room. As other students and faculty
members waited for lunch, drinking sherry and speculat-
ing about the new semester, Loring and I discussed my
treatments. My next chemo was in one week and Loring
had just heard that I had swum two miles that morning. He
was not amused.

"There's no papal bull on what to do," he began, "and
since your cancer is so incredibly rare, some of our sugges-
tions are arbitrary. But certain facts do exist. Chemo pro-
tocol can insult the bone marrow and cause a cumulative
cardiotoxic effect." As Loring talked Debby drifted by, rea-
lized what we were talking about, and quickly departed.

"Herb, I think you're overestimating your endurance,"
Loring continued. "And you're disregarding the chemical's
influence. You're definitely under an acute influence of
chemo agents. They can quickly sap your strength and
physical reserve. Now, it's not my personality to be rigid,
but I am nervous about your sports level." Loring reached
for the sherry and carefully poured a small amount. "Are
you planning on doing this for much longer?"

I still felt elated after the long swim. I had probably
never swum two miles before. I had been wondering

whether sports, besides providing a psychological boost, could help my body absorb the chemicals. Could a lower level of stress, a stronger heart, and lower weight help a cancer patient? My medical knowledge equalled that of the *National Enquirer,* but I couldn't let that realization bother me.

I turned to Loring. "Let's see how I do next week," I suggested. If things go better than last month, I'll do more sports."

Loring studied me. The ball was out of his court. As Dean Whitlock called us for lunch, Loring ruefully remarked, "You're crazy. You really are, Herb."

Senior Common Room wasn't the only aspect of Dudley House that I appreciated. The kitchen employees and secretaries knew about my cancer ("we certainly talked a lot about it," recalls the Master's secretary) but they treated it diffidently with me.

Miriam is a middle-aged cashier who devours Gothic novels while living for her annual Las Vegas or Honolulu vacations. I never realized that Miriam knew about my cancer until her cash register once stuck as she was ringing up my breakfast.

"Damn it," she snapped. Then, looking at me she concluded "I've got a no-good machine and you've got cancer. Ain't life a bummer?"

Whereas dining hall managers of other houses pride themselves on maintaining a traditional decorum, Ronnie takes an amusingly independent tack. In his mid-forties, with red hair and a paunch, Ronnie delights in displaying a large original Disney painting of Micky Mouse in Dudley's dining room. Doling out equally large amounts of free coffee and off-color jokes, he is one of Harvard's most popular employees.

After running down from Porter Square on a wintry afternoon I stopped in at Dudley for a bowl of Ronnie's pungent chili. Ronnie stared at my head which had always been adorned with a full complement of hair—natural, or otherwise.

"Hey, something's really wrong with you, isn't it?" he asked.

"Cancer," I responded with the same tone as when revealing a joke's punch line.

"That's what I heard." Obviously relieved that I could admit it, Ronnie offered, "Have a cigarette? And we got a good shipment of Tab in this morning; good year for Tab; there was sufficient rain." As I walked over to a grinning Debby and Brian, he yelled after me. "And there's always some hamburgers and hotdogs packed with healthy nitrites. Hey, whaddya got against my place, anyway?"

Halfway through chemo I was discovering that many more people than I had suspected knew about my cancer, and that their initial hesitation (and our mutual discomfort) could usually be eliminated by an offhand remark about my cancer (never "my illness"), chemotherapy, or my perpetually mobile wig. A discussion of cancer would reveal both the concern and curiosity of my friends. Confidences, I discovered, quickly led to other confidences.

One snowy evening as I walked with Debby back from dinner I mentioned that the other tutors rarely asked me about cancer and chemo. "Sometimes, like the night before chemo, it's just really difficult keeping it all inside me. I wish they'd feel free to talk about it."

"Oh, they're interested in you all right," Debby responded. "Every evening when I come in they ask about you. Was Herb sick today, how many miles did he run, anything new on his chances? But they're just as uncertain whether to talk about it as you are. Somebody's got to give and then it'll be okay."

I thought for a moment. "But you and I are good friends and yet I've always felt that you clam up whenever I talk about cancer. If you're that way, then I hate to think how other people will react."

Debby didn't say anything for a long while. I wondered whether she had heard me. I was about to repeat myself when she haltingly said, "I think I'm that way because I've always worried about dying from cancer. Cancer killed my

mother and I'm overweight which means I'm susceptible
and I use a lot of hairdye which is supposed to be car-
cinogenic and so when I see you—hell, you don't smoke or
use hairdye and you've never been overweight in your life
but now you've got it and things don't look so good . . ."
Debby's voice trailed off. She silently took my hand and we
walked back to Apley.

I could have done without some of the solicitude. Mrs.
R was a widow who owned a cottage near Danvers. For sev-
eral years we had known each other casually and recently
we had discussed my chemo difficulties. As I was lying in
Stillman, waiting for my December chemo, she called me
and invited me over for tobogganing.

We spent a pleasant three hours skimming down
freshly powdered hills and then tugging the sled back up.
On the first run the wind had snatched my wig and skicap
from my head. As we continued flying down the hill, Mrs.
R screamed that we should stop and pick up the wig. I
grinned and yelled back that we had to complete the run. A
skier retrieved my accouterments. I thought the incident
was mildly amusing. Mrs. R, on the other hand, was clearly
puzzled by my attitude and was concerned that I might
catch a cold.

As we conversed over a sumptuous roast beef and wine
dinner, Mrs. R expressed a marked concern about my fam-
ily's reaction to my cancer. By nine o'clock we were loung-
ing in front of the fire when she suddenly put down her
wine glass and touched my knee.

"Do you have a special girlfriend who's helping you?"
she inquired.

I looked at Mrs R's fortyish face, as the light from the
fire turned her hair even more red than usual. I replied that,
while I had several close women friends, nobody was spe-
cial.

She slid closer and, moving her hand up my leg, said "It
shouldn't be like that." I shrugged, as if accepting the arbi-
trary ordering of the universe. She stroked my wig and
then murmured "You're so nice and I do feel sorry for you."

Even lacking recent experience, I now realized that Mrs. R was attempting her level best to seduce me. Given normal circumstances I might have reciprocated. But the chemo's effect on my libido coupled with my better assumption that it was only from pity she was offering her favors.

I tried to pull away. She held me tighter and shook her head. "It's snowing outside. You should stay here tonight. I've got a very big bed."

I hurriedly offered numerous explanations why I had to return to Cambridge. When I concluded, she pursed her lips. "Has it—you know—the cancer, has it made you not like girls anymore?"

Acknowledging a rebuff to my male ego, I nodded my head. "Yes," I morosely reflected. "That's one of the worst parts about chemo."

"Damn. I wish there's something I could do for you." She paused and look at me expectantly. But I felt much the same as when my friend had offered me five dollars when hearing about my cancer. I thanked Mrs. R for her consideration. A few minutes later I was driving home.

I continued to disregard the note cards and scattered outlines of my thesis as I pursued my athletics. I had ten days before my February chemo. Loring had negotiated with me until I agreed to do nothing athletic for forty-eight hours prior to entering Stillman.

On Monday I ran down to the Museum of Science with Danny. A month earlier, when I realized that we would be running fairly often together, I mentioned the cancer, while stressing that a moderate sports program could benefit me. But as we passed the M.I.T. boathouse, which marks the halfway point to the museum, Danny started yelling at me.

"Okay, we all know you're macho. But now you're being an asshole. Stop this shit, will ya?" I turned around and politely suggested that he really should refrain from using my cancer as an excuse for any shortcomings. "Fuckin' A,"

Danny cursed as he started running harder. When I arrived home a postcard from my father mentioned that he had just won the national championship in the 400-meter freestyle for his age group.

On Monday I was pummelling the heavy bag when the class of black Tae Kwon Doists swaggered in. I looked over, blinked away some sweat, and waved to them. My first encounter with them had raised my spirits. Now, as the students warmed up, their instructor came over and quietly studied me.

"How about going a couple of rounds?" I asked. I had enjoyed the last time, I added, and had been working out regularly.

The teacher nodded. "You're going through some medical thing, aren't you?"

"Yeah. Something called chemotherapy."

"That's what I thought," he responded. "Nothing personal, okay? But I don't want to box with you." He turned around and walked back to his class. Suddenly he turned and, with a wide grin, yelled "Hey, good luck. Y'hear?"

On the last day of workouts before chemo I swam twenty "no breathers" (going a length without breathing, taking several gulps of air, and then starting back). Then, after a mile of freestyle, I changed and ran upstairs to the weightroom. I wanted to make every minute count. Saying "hi" to the blind weightlifter, I slid 140 pounds and two weight collars onto the bar.

As I pressed the bar I thought ahead to the Cooperstown race. "Shit, I'm in better shape than last year. I know that I can finish. I want to win that race." And as I curled eighty pounds I thought of the three portages: behind Bassett Hospital, climbing up and down the steep hill at Goodyear Lake, and then the three hundred yards at the dam in Oneonta. The most troublesome area was Goodyear. The portage was up and then down a steep hill and several canoeists had plummeted over the dam.

Classical music from the weightlifter's tape recorder

floated around the room as I grunted and continued to think about the race. Winning, placing, or even finishing with a good time would nicely conclude this crazy year. I disassembled the bar, bid goodby to the weightlifter, and bounced out into the frosty night air. As I walked home, I passed a bar where middle-aged men had grouped around a television to watch a Boston Celtics game. Thinking of how athletics were helping me, I wondered whether the flickering images inside the bar weren't a modern version of Plato's shadows from the cave.

On Thursday I visited Paula Williams, whom I had first met two months earlier. Her doctors had already informed her of her probable death. But she insisted on rising early in the morning and painfully walking around the corner for the newspaper. At home she spent most of her hours designing and constructing intricate mobiles. She transformed her bedroom and then the dining room and hallway into a menagerie of swooping, soaring seagulls. Paula had always loved the sea. During her first weeks of radiation she would walk for hours along Nantucket's shore. At first she could walk alone but later only with Jack's increasing help. Eventually her body couldn't endure the five-hour trip from Boston to Nantucket.

Each time I visited Paula she had cursed her growing inability to walk and, later, her difficulty in stringing seagulls onto mobile thread. "I've still got the will," she had said recently, "but I'm sure losing the way." During my last visit I had to carry all fifty-five pounds of her across the room.

On Thursday a next-door neighbor let me in; Paula could not manage stairs. After we ate the dinner I had cooked, we sat in the living room where we sipped wine and compared our different methods of coping with cancer.

"I need somebody else. Without Jack I simply couldn't handle this," Paula began. "Even more than loving him, I trust him. He knows me like nobody else and he'll always be around. Everything else around here is changing. We've moved a lot since we married. And people fall in and out of our lives by graduating, dropping out, not getting tenure, or breaking up a relationship. And now, my cancer has created problems most other people don't realize. Like how to deal with people, how to plan whatever future you've got left, and how to reconcile yourself to not having children."

Leaning back on the sofa, Paula winced and haltingly fingered her wine glass. "But it's strange that you're doing well without somebody really close. Without any special somebody you can run like hell and not worry about somebody nagging you later." Paula looked at me and tried to smile. "I never would've thought of trying it your way. Yet, I'm still here because of Jack and you're still here maybe because you don't have anybody."

Later that night I sat in front of the fireplace, gazing idly at the flames and speculating how well I would respond to the new chemo. Conant and Grey had warned that the impact would be greater. "But you've only got to go through one day instead of two," Loring had offered.

From the stereo Joan Baez was singing "Take this ribbon from my hair, shake it loose and let it fall. All I'm asking is your time. Help me make it through the night." I thought over the last six months, to my reaction when Dunn told me that I had cancer, to Claudia and our last night together when she convinced me that I could do anything I wanted.

I thumbed through the posters of the lecturers I had brought to Dudley and remembered how, a day after December's chemo, I had trooped through snowdrifts to tack up over a hundred posters announcing a talk by Professor Hoffman. "How'd you get all these people here?" a puzzled Hoffman had asked later.

I nervously paced through my living room and into the bedroom. A large color photo showed Charlie and me starting the Cooperstown race. As we had paddled to the starting line both of us had felt pain in our upper backs from last-minute practice. "You really think we're going to finish?" I asked Charlie. But we had kept going and, upon finishing, our pride made any physical soreness irrelevant.

I thought of teaching at Maine, writing my thesis, teaching at Harvard, work at Dudley, and my increasing athletics. "I've done everything well," I decided. "That is, everything but chemo." Tomorrow would give me the chance to prove the wisdom of my sports schedule.

"Herb, your white count is down again." The nurse was in the final stage of preparing the IV tree when Loring walked in. "Three days ago, a good 5.4. Down to a 3.9 ten days ago. And now you're at 3.4." Shaking his head Loring said, "I don't need to tell you that if you get too tired from sports then we could have a real problem—infections and having to delay chemo." I nodded and said that I felt fine. Looking at the chemo vials and tubing, I felt an equal mixture of hate and respect.

Tight-lipped, Loring started the new protocol. Two nurses stood in the corner. An icepack, to lessen burning, lay flopped over my right wrist.

Ten minutes later, as the DTIC began trickling down, Loring looked inquiringly at me. The drug was burning my arm and I felt unusually tired. But I attributed the latter feeling to tension. Inwardly I smiled, happy that I had only once asked to have the flow halted.

I wondered how doctors were capable of treating dying patients, sleeping well at night, and then coming back the next day. Dr. Greenwalter, who had assisted me through radiation, would retreat to an unused hospital room whenever possible and practice his banjo. Loring had spoken of his wife and two children as "reminders of hope. They give me the buoyancy to bounce back. And music is very nourishing. If I'm really depressed, I'll play the recorder. Either that or I'll split wood. Sometimes when I'm really bugging my family, we'll all play a game called Quadruple Canfield. It's great for releasing frustrations harmlessly."

I was jarred back to the present as Loring asked "How're things going?"

A chemo patient usually talks with clipped sentences

during chemo. Not only is he tense and the doctor busy, but the patient never really knows when he will be sick. I looked at Loring and tried to grin. "It's okay. I guess I'll be sick. But later. And we expect that anyway, right?"

Loring nodded absently and watched the DTIC slowly drip down the five feet of transparent tubing. A few minutes later he breathed a heavy sigh of relief. The nurse uncoupled the bottles and tubing and placed them in the cart.

"I'm glad. And, a little surprised that it went so well," Loring commented. "But let's not stretch our luck. Get some good sleep tonight and then stay here as long as you want tomorrow." He looked at my t-shirt with Johnnie's beatific grin on it. "And please, no more histrionics like last time. The Emergency Ward nurses get tired of seeing the same old faces."

I vomited four times within an hour of his leaving. "Oh, Jesus," I muttered while struggling back to bed, "they really hit me this time." A nurse came in and helped me back. But at that moment I smelled Harvard's version of Mystery Meat wafting down the hall.

"I don't think I'm very hungry," I informed the nurse while starting to gag. She guided me back to the bathroom, where she stood patiently as I vomited once more. Finally, tucking me into bed she said "You did just fine today." I smiled politely and fell asleep within a few minutes.

For the first time in several months I slept well over eight hours. At nine o'clock, as I still lay sleeping, Jane came by, the first friend to visit me in chemo.

As she recalls, "It was a dreary, cold, typically Boston day of fog and rain. I knew you hated to have friends come but I decided 'I'm going anyway just to see you.' The nurses immediately knew who I wanted. You were in a deep REM sleep. I whispered but you didn't answer. Then I started talking louder and louder until I was afraid nurses would think there was an argument. So I started shaking you and slamming cabinet doors. As I shook you I remember thinking, 'I want you to wake up. I want to tell you that you're okay.' But you wouldn't wake up. Maybe you were compensating for all those other nights. So, I just stood and looked at you for about twenty minutes. I let a lot of thoughts bicycle through my mind; how unprepared I was for your joking about cancer, how you had joked when telling me that you'd lost your thesis. And how I wanted you, and my sister, and Miriam to get well. And, as usual, I wondered where your mother was. I finally left and wandered into my favorite bookstore. I didn't want to see anybody or anything."

At ten o'clock, having slept fourteen hours, I wearily opened my eyes. A huge red object hovered menacingly above me. I rubbed my eyes and saw a collection of tulips thrust inside my water pitcher. Attached to the stems was a card. "Herb, we all love you. But next time, wake up when somebody visits you. Love. Jane."

# Seven

"DAMN IT, HERB, you're blowing it." Loring angrily cast the CBC report aside and turned to me. For the last two weeks I had ignored a persistent cough and had been running more than before. Spring, the possible completion of chemo, the canoe race, and the end of school now seemed within my grasp.

But now Loring was telling me, "You've got to cut the sports out. Last week,"—Loring consulted his notes—"March ninth, you had a 2.8 white count and so you couldn't take chemo and I told you to take it easy. But today we've got another 2.8." Loring smiled wanly at me. "Now I'm not going to sermonize but we're two weeks behind the protocol. This delay, if you continue it, could be dangerous."

I had never seen Loring upset before; his demeanor expressed the medical seriousness. I reluctantly nodded agreement—no more sports for the next week.

At my office better news greeted me. A two-sentence letter from Blue Cross notifying me that it would accept practically all of my medical expenses. I quickly embraced my luck. Any questioning, I assumed, could reverse the decision.

To replace my running and squash I increased my student tutorials. Like my nieces and nephews, the students offered relief from my medical worries. This year I had expressed less concern about exams and grades while enjoying my students more. When I was an undergraduate, my African history teacher had sat with me for several hours in a college bar and evaluated my term paper line by line. The actual subject matter became unimportant. His attention and criticisms taught me how to write and organize my thoughts. I had resolved to follow his example but I kept postponing doing so, claiming that my thesis had top priority. Now I knew that I might not have another chance.

I surprised myself by quickly mentioning my low blood count to Debby, Jon, and Jane. They applauded my abstinence from sports and during the following week would call daily or drop by to show their support.

The next Wednesday Debby and I walked over to the infirmary where I had a white blood count of 4400. I still approached chemo with a tense reluctance. Familiarity had not bred contempt. I knew how debilitating Cytoxan, Adriamycin and DTIC could be. Increasingly, however, I prided myself on having struggled, however unheroically, through previous chemo sessions. Having fought chemo's side effects for so long, I couldn't give up now. Thursday's chemo produced the usual vomiting.

Belatedly, I realized an unintentional effect of my friends' solicitousness. On Thursday evening I wrote to my parents, ". . . by now most acquaintances know at least part of my story and I quietly try to combat expressions of commiseration and health advice by doing more than I otherwise would." On Friday afternoon I played baseball on a still snowy field.

"You've got one more chemo date before we renegotiate." Loring leaned back in his chair and brushed a fallen comma of red-brown hair back into position.

"Your last session was okay. Better than I expected. But now I hear you're doing more sports. I suppose

I should read you the Riot Act, but . . ." His voice trailed off
as he gave me an exasperated look.

As spring hesitantly skirted Cambridge in early April, I
was spending most of my days outside and working on my
thesis at night. In January, sports had persuaded me that
with sufficient willpower I could stretch my physical limits.
With that assumption I agreed to take more chemo. As I
completed the six-months' protocol I knew that I could
finish my thesis if I worked as hard as I had along the
Charles or in my room at Stillman. Already I had recon-
structed the one-hundred-twenty pages I had burned in
January.

For several days Professor Williams had been suggest-
ing that I visit Paula. On a Wednesday in mid-April we
drove across town to Deaconess Hospital. Williams ap-
peared distraught and spoke haltingly. He resembled a ner-
vous graduate student before an important exam more
than a tenured Harvard professor.

"She's giving in, Herb," he said. "Doesn't go out much
anymore. Doesn't see her friends except when they drop
by. She's eating next to nothing. And the only time she
shows any guts, and spirit, is when she demands pain med-
ication." Jack shook his head hopelessly. "I thought I knew
my wife. Six weeks ago I couldn't imagine my Paula giving
in. I just don't want to see her go out like this. Maybe you
can help."

Paula's hospital room was almost completely dark. As
Jack tugged at the curtains I noticed that plants sent by
Paula's friends had begun to turn yellow. Paula lay flat and
unmoving, her matchstick legs sticking out from her john-
nie. Clumps of hair lay on her sheet and pillow. As I moved
closer, she gazed at me with the weary tolerance shown by
dying patients to their solicitous friends.

Jack began pacing the room, criticizing his wife's in-
creased reliance on such pain-killing barbiturates as De-
merol and Dilaudid. In a rising, impassioned voice Jack ar-
gued that her drug usage was denying any chance of liv-
ing.

Finally halting at the foot of Paula's bed, Jack began chronicling how I had never given up hope. His praise discomforted me. Paula was dying and I stood a good chance of living. Feeling like an intruder in her domain, I shifted uneasily as Jack grabbed my shoulder. "Look at Herb, Paula. *He* made it."

As Paula continued to look resignedly at her husband, Jack lowered his voice. "Baby, you've got to stop taking all these drugs. Try to fight. You shouldn't die like this. Maybe we can win. But we'll never know unless you try."

Paula's response was to cough violently, her frail body shaking with each wheeze. Finally, with her voice breaking she half-whispered "Jack, we've been through all this. I don't enjoy eating and you sure as hell don't know the pain I'm in." Tears flowed down her cheeks and onto the crisp hospital sheets. "Oh, God" she began sobbing. "I've been a bad wife. I'm sorry, Jack. I'm dying on you. And I'm taking you away from your work. I guess I've been a bad investment; you'll be paying bills for a long time after I die." Paula stopped temporarily and blew her nose. Glancing apologetically at me she said, "I'm sorry."

Later, in the hallway, I asked Jack how much longer Paula would live.

He gazed down the corridor. Nurses were busily wheeling patients onto the sunporch where they could enjoy one of Cambridge's rare sunny days. Jack shook his head in resignation. "I don't know, Herb. I just don't know."

"But she is going to die?"

Jack hesitated for a moment. "Yes, but the point is this. If Paula gives in now, both she and I'll lose respect for her." Adjusting his glasses, Jack looked at me. "I love Paula. But I also want to respect her. These are her last days. They're her final chance to show everybody what a really fine person she is." Jack's voice caught and he shrugged hopelessly.

"I'm really lost," he continued. "Should I keep holding on by encouraging her to eat and not take those damn pills or should I let go? The Demerol and the morphine

make her feel better and I should like that. But if she takes
those drugs and doesn't eat, then she'll lose any notion of
self-reliance, any chance of beating cancer. The drugs turn
her into a zombie, and if she doesn't eat she'll be dead
within the week."

Taking me by the shoulder, Jack said "If I give in to her,
it'll be out of character for me. I wouldn't like doing that
and she'd know that I had given up on her. You do see that,
don't you?"

I nodded. But as the two of us walked over to the hospi-
tal's parking lot, I wondered whether Jack wasn't thrusting
his own personality onto that of his dying wife.

A few days later Jack called me to ask if I could meet
him at Deaconess. As we walked down the faded yellow
hallway, Jack commented, "Paula's in really bad shape.
She's lost another three pounds since you saw her. She's
just below fifty pounds. Herb, for the first time I'm really
scared. Paula's going to die!"

I looked at my friend. Under his arm were textbooks
and papers. He was unshaven, his eyes seemed bright red,
and his normally well-combed hair was a mess. For the last
four days he had received permission to stay overnight in
Paula's room.

We approached Paula's open door. I could hear her
speaking rapidly, breathlessly to a nurse. The pillows
needed fluffing, she wanted more water, and where were
the pills which the doctor had said that she could have?

As we entered Paula took one look at me. "I want Jack,
Jack alone." The nurse and I left. As we stepped out I could
hear Paula's soft sobbing.

Paula had especially liked the heavy-set, black nurse.
"How is she?" I asked. But as the nurse started to answer
we heard Paula plead quietly, "Help me, help me. Move me
over. Oh, God. Please don't leave me, please don't leave me,
please don't . . ." The nurse glanced at me, slowly shook
her head, and then looked away. "Poor kid," she muttered.

Half an hour later Jack emerged and silently walked

with me to the cafeteria. He appeared both exhausted and subdued. Finally he said, "She's given in. There's nothing left of the fighter I married ten years ago. But she's too far down the road for me to worry anymore. I guess I've been too hard on her. Now, all I can do is hold her and wait."

We entered the food line but Jack shook his head. "I can't eat. We're sitting here while some goddamn giant timer is counting off the seconds." He rested his head upon his hands. "I just hope that I've been a good husband," he finally said.

Spring events were inevitably jamming against each other. I scheduled unpopular additional classes in African politics. I was also striving to finish a rough draft of two hundred thesis pages. And I was running more than ever before. Cooperstown was only a month away.

On April 26th and 27th I had three speakers at Dudley House. On the 28th, with ten-hours' notice, I presented a short talk at a national conference on the U.S. and Africa. When I finished speaking, a fellow Dudley student drove me to the airport to meet Sam Brown, President Carter's appointee to head ACTION. As we threaded our way through Boston's traffic, I dashed off an introduction to Brown. It was a rhapsodic speech that everyone enjoyed. Everyone, except Sam Brown. He interrupted me halfway through my oration with the whispered plea, "Can't we cut this crap short?"

After Brown's talk I hurried through the Yard to attend receptions for visiting congressmen and diplomats. Frankly, I enjoyed mixing with big names, since it shoved aside my usual preoccupation with cancer. The next morning I woke late and sprinted to Adams House for another conference. Fortunately, someone had saved me a seat. Out of breath I sat down.

Hoping that nobody could hear my panting, I looked around and found that I was sitting between Jacqueline Onassis and Caroline Kennedy. While a journalist speculated on the new Carter presidency I scanned the packed room and thought "Here I am with Jody Powell, the Kennedys, and God knows who else and after this conference we'll hobnob like good friends. Maybe it'll seem glamorous. But next Tuesday I'll be alone in Stillman's green-tiled bathroom, vomiting like crazy and these celebrities will be nowhere to be seen. I'm going through something most of them have never experienced."

As the meeting ended, Mrs. Onassis turned and studied my name tag. "It's Herb, is it? How are you doing?"

"Just fine," I laughed, "just fine."

As I strolled to Stillman on Tuesday I remembered my first chemo and how easy it had initially seemed. And then the increasing pain and sleepless nights, the January breakdown followed by my sports. Today, being possibly my last session, somehow seemed like a graduation.

My radio began playing Handel's "Water Music." Smiling from behind the IV tubing, Laurie asked "Is that for the chemo or for your canoe race?" I smiled back and thought of how Loring had suggested that classical music could help me relax during chemotherapy.

A few minutes later, just after Loring had started the Cytoxan, I suddenly grunted involuntarily. Gastric juice started seeping into my mouth. Loring looked up. I frantically pointed at a green basin. Loring flicked off the flow valve. Laurie placed the bedpan under my mouth as I coughed up my breakfast of pancakes and yogurt.

"Oh, shit!" I exclaimed. As Laurie wiped the remaining vomit spittle off my chin, I looked at her and Loring. "I'm sorry." I said.

"There's nothing to be sorry about," replied Loring. "Do you want to rest?"

"Nope. Let's finish in a hurry."

But a few minutes later I again vomited. As Laurie wiped away, I grinned. "Let's have another go," I said.

Reluctantly Loring flipped the flow valve and watched

the Adriamycin inch towards my wrist. I lay back as the gastric juice subsided. The classical music began soothing me.

A few minutes later, as Loring inserted the DTIC syringe into the clear tubing, he looked down at me. "This is the last time I can speak to you without you walking out on me," he smiled. He watched the DTIC bottle empty and I suspected that he was deciding what to say about the canoe race.

"You're taking chemo a lot better. And you look a lot better," he offered. "But your body's going to need time and rest." Loring paused. "I hope you've reconsidered your decision about the race. I think it could be dangerous."

There was a blue sky outside and sun streamed through my hospital window. A seagull, sunning itself on the roof, suddenly spread its wings and flew away. Students darting towards the Charles were flicking frisbees as they ran. Turning to Conant I replied, "I'm going ahead with Cooperstown. I think I can do it. And if I can't, well, at least I will have tried."

Loring had finished packing the chemo equipment. Standing at the foot of the bed with arms folded, he admitted "I can't hold you back. But if you do go, take it easy. I mean it. Don't get so hopped up that you chase every canoe. And stop along the way if you get tired. Otherwise, you'll seriously damage yourself." He tilted his head back and looked at me. "Agreed?" he inquired.

"Agreed," I solemnly replied. Immediately after Loring left I ran towards the bathroom. I started vomiting as I entered. Two hours later I limped back to bed. As I quickly fell asleep I realized that spring's chemo was acting faster and affecting me worse than the fall sessions. Yet compared to the November and December chemos, psychologically I felt less upset. Chemo was becoming old hat.

On Wednesday morning I finally did what I had often thought of doing during the last six months. During several chemo sessions at Stillman my breakfast nurse had appeared visibly nervous whenever I was around. "She probably frets about having a dying cancer patient on her hands," I had suggested to Debby.

I awoke with the sun. Soon the breakfast carts began clanking down the hallway. Still tasting the remains of nausea I nevertheless grinned as I stumbled towards the closet. I pulled out my Ape-Face.

Back in bed I slipped the rubberband attachment over my head and then pulled the blue blanket over my head. The breakfast nurse soon entered. Looking down at the lumpy blanket, she uncertainly inquired "Mr. Howe, are you awake?"

No response from the lump. Again, "Mr. Howe, it's time to get up." Finally, she testily said "It's breakfast and you're required to eat it."

I bit my lip to avoid laughing. I could feel her getting closer and closer. Finally the magic moment as she pulled my blanket away.

"Oh, shit. Oh, my God. Oh, no" she yelled and ran from the room. I smiled and lay back in the bed. I had scored another victory against passivity and dependence.

On the Sunday before I left for Cooperstown I ran for an hour, swam, worked three hours on my thesis, and then attended the Boston Pops with other students. After the concert I threw a spontaneous birthday party for Debby in my suite. As one of my closer friends, Debby hadn't retreated from my cancer but had constantly offered unflagging support. When the last of the celebrants finally left, I gratefully fell into bed. As I drifted into sleep I thought of the recent busy days and the Cooperstown race. Life had never seemed so rewarding.

At nine o'clock the next morning the phone's ringing cut short my sleep. Stumbling across the room, I speculated about the identity of this miscreant.

"Herb, she's dead."

It was Jack. Suddenly I was wide awake.

"Paula died at two-thirty this morning. I was sitting by her bed. She turned to look at me. 'Hold me, Jack' she said. We kissed and a few minutes later, her head it just slumped forward. I held her for a long time. God, I felt alone. Then I got up. I had to tell the nurses."

Jack mentioned that during the last two days Paula had become more and more muddled, waving at unseen people and often imagining herself back in Scotland where she had once spent a satisfying semester.

"I knew then that she was going to die soon and that she should have whatever I could give her. All my ideas about resistance and pride didn't mean anything anymore. I loved her and this was the last time I could help her."

We talked for an hour. Jack was leaving soon for Paula's parents in Connecticut. We promised to keep in touch once he returned.

With Cooperstown now three days away I pushed aside all thoughts of Dudley, my classes, and my thesis. I devoted myself to running, swimming, and lifting weights. I called Lin to tell her when I would arrive. She had been frantically packing furniture and attending to the innumerable small details of moving a family across country. On the day after the race she, Charlie, and the three kids would drive out to Wisconsin where Charlie had received a new parish.

"I want to see you, brother, but I'm not feeling kindly about the race. Charlie's more interested in racing than moving. I'll have him call you back."

On Thursday Grey and I briefly discussed possible future treatments. He advocated more chemo, stressing that any side effects were relatively unimportant compared to the chance that I still might have cancer. I replied that I would wait until completing the canoe race before deciding whether to continue.

After talking to Grey I noticed that it was only ten o'clock. I impulsively walked to Peter Bent Brigham's radiation ward. Down the same yellow halls and past elderly patients gazing vacantly from their wheelchairs. No longer a patient, I now noticed their almost exaggerated politeness: everyone's reluctance to enter the elevator first, men giving their seats to women in the waiting rooms, open affection shown by old people to children they had never met. And, elderly black and white men chatting contentedly together. They could have been bitter enemies in their youth but now they appeared the best of friends.

Against any reasonable odds I saw Miss Marple. She was bending over a nurses' station where she was rustling a bundle of blue and white insurance forms. Next to her was a framed stained glass with the suggestion "Along the Way Take Time to Smell the Flowers." I smiled, wondering whether Miss Marple had given the glass to the hospital.

It had been three months since I had last seen her. As I approached, I assumed that I'd have to reintroduce myself. But as she turned around, her eyes widened. Delightedly she grabbed me.

"*Where* have you been? We missed you. You know, it's not nice to leave just like that without telling anyone. But enough, enough. How is life?"

She nodded gravely as I sketched in the last few months of chemotherapy, my breakdown, and my sports.

"You're doing well, I think." Miss Marple studied me. "Don't lose sight of the forest through the trees. You're on the right path. Don't let the little obstacles fool you."

I smiled appreciatively and asked about the radiation patients.

"Well," she paused while searching for the right words. "Arthur, my husband, died over Christmas. It's sad; we had two plane tickets for Miami, but he passed away two days before. At home. He insisted on that. 'No hospitals,' he said. 'I want to die where I lived and I want to know that you'll be with me when I die.' " Miss Marple paused and busied herself by folding the insurance forms and neatly placing them in her bag.

"You know," she continued, "both of us knew that Arthur would soon die. I'd been living with it for four years.

You can never really prepare yourself for it. But we've got to do our best."

I offered to walk her to the bus and as we crossed Commonwealth Avenue she started telling me about Gloria.

"Somehow we all knew that when Gloria started chemotherapy and lost those golden curls, she was going to die," Miss Marple recalled. "But the real kicker was, well, remember how she used to kick and scream when the attendants came into the waiting room? After she started chemo she'd walk by herself. No protest. Down the hall to the radiation machine. No crying, nothing. Then she'd come back, not say anything, and leave with her mother. I hated to hear her scream but I guess she still had some fight left. The last month, well, it was like one long funeral. She died two weeks before my Arthur."

Miss Marple shivered and pulled her overcoat tighter. She looked remarkably healthy for a terminally ill patient. "Gloria and Arthur," she reflected. "I guess none of us had much Christmas spirit."

She grabbed my hand as the green and white trolley approached. "You've still got a chance. You mustn't blow it. Keep running. If you ever slow down, you'll be in trouble. Remember us, Good-by."

I watched her trundle up the trolley steps and felt incredibly close to her. I've never seen her since.

On Thursday Charlie called. "You are still racing with me, aren't you?" After I assured him, he explained the race. The aluminum class, which is the slowest, would be leaving at six in the morning. Our class, the amateur racers, would depart an hour later. And the professionals, who were competing for a first prize of over a thousand dollars, would leave at eight. "Is anyone going to be watching this fiasco?" I asked, trying to recall last year's race.

The Chamber of Commerce claims there's usually about seventy-five thousand along the route," replied Charlie.

"Man Attacks Dog As Wife Sues For Alimony." Huddling over the *Boston Globe,* one hand absently encircling a styrofoam coffee cup, I immersed myself in the sport of monitoring the world's crazies. Knowing that Planet Earth housed individuals who prided themselves on setting world records for pizza consumption allowed me to place in its proper porportions my battle against cancer. In one day I would leave for Cooperstown.

A hand gripped my shoulder and Dean Whitlock, Master of Dudley House, sat down. After exchanging the usual pleasantries, Whitlock grew serious.

"You won't be with us next year, I understand. And, we'll miss you. You've done a great job under trying circumstances." Whitlock stared at the coffee cup. "Debby and Brian tell me that you're going through with this half-assed canoe race of yours and that there's nobody who can stop you." He glanced up. "Is that right?"

"Yes," I said and added that I hoped he wouldn't try to convince me otherwise. He smiled and adjusted his wire-rimmed spectacles.

"Would if I could, but I'm not even going to try. I'll just wish you the best of luck."

# Eight

FROM THE ROLLING HILLS at Farmers' Museum to Super Suicide and Heartbreak hills by Bassett Hospital, Cooperstown had burst out in a luxuriant green. The deer had returned to the deer park, where they chewed on clumps of grass nervously held by grinning children. At Cooperstown High School seniors lolled around and talked about next year. On Main Street kids sprinted towards the Baseball Hall of Fame, their gloves carefully strung on the belts of their blue jeans.

Some of the best canoe racers and racing equipment in North America had invaded Cooperstown. Four-wheel-drive jeeps cruised along the town's narrow streets carrying sleek racing canoes: Jensen cedar strips, Sawyer Kevlars, and Mad River Malecites. License plates from Ontario, Quebec, Minnesota, Michigan, and Washington indicated the race's reputation. Over one-hundred-fifty people from Athol, a small Massachusetts town, had arrived as members and friends of Athol's Rat Pack.

Cooperstown's spring vibrancy reflected my own mood. The harsh winter had at last retreated, surrendering to a period of growth and expectation. For the last several weeks I had been waiting for the Cooperstown race as the culmination of events that had begun almost a year earlier with the operation, Claudia, and my return to Harvard.

As Lin and her children greeted me at the Albany bus station she announced, "I haven't prepared anything for tonight. Vinia, Willie, and John insisted that I give you *carte blanche* to prepare tonight's salad." A few hours later, after the children and I had gone shopping, the five Paysons and I greedily consumed an expensive salad.

Charlie and I discussed the race. No, he hadn't put in more than ten hours of practice. No, the paddles weren't quite ready but would be finished by the race.

More competitors had entered and many, perhaps most, would be using the lightweight racing canoes. Recent breakthroughs in material and design had prompted manufacturers to produce canoes weighing as little as thirty pounds. In comparison, the standard aluminum canoe weighs eighty pounds. The new racing canoes have a narrow beam, or width, a tapered bow and stern, and a small freeboard, the distance from the top of the canoe to the top of the water. The racing canoes are built from Fiberglas, cedar, or Kevaar (a lightweight material also used to produce bulletproof vests). Charlie and I did not have such a state-of-the-art craft. We would be paddling an eighty-pound, ten-year-old Fiberglas family canoes.

"That's not all the bad news," Charlie added. The river is really low this year. Some people say it's the lowest they've seen it for this time of year."

Realizing that the race would remain The Topic, Vinia and Co. scooped up the remains of the salad and left, knocking over several packing crates. As Lin cleared the dishes, Charlie spread a topographic map of the river upon the table.

He looked at me as I studied the map. "The Lincoln has a hull speed of about six knots," he said. "We'd need a motor to go faster. If we're good, we should finish in about thirteen hours. But here are some ways we can lower our time." Charlie bent over and pointed to Otsego Lake. "First, we've got to get a good start at Otsego. We'll practice that tomorrow morning. I guess you remember the portages behind Bassett Hospital, Goodyear Lake, and Oneonta. They'll be tough. And then there's the Swamp. It's close to here. We'll do that tomorrow afternoon."

The Swamp is a narrow, ten-mile section of the Susque-hanna river coursing through forest and thick vegetation. Stumps lurk just below the water while large branches lie a few feet above the surface. Knowledge of these and other obstacles in the race is essential if canoeists plan to make good time without capsizing or ripping their canoes apart.

But the obvious challenge of the seventy-two mile race is endurance. A canoeist must maintain a steady pace of at least sixty strokes per minute while not tiring himself out prematurely.

As Charlie and I continued talking, Lin sorted out various family belongings and placed them in cartons. Eventually she sat down with us and poured a glass of wine. Looking at me, she asked "How do you feel about doing the seventy-two?"

I grinned, first at her and then Charlie. "If your out-of-shape husband will just guide the boat, I'll paddle both of us in."

"You really feel healthy enough to compete?" persisted Lin.

"Yes."

The next morning Charlie and I inspected the canoe, loaded it onto his car, and drove the half mile to Otsego Lake.

Once in the water Charlie quickly explained the first four strokes of the race, strokes which we hoped would sep-arate us quickly from the pack.

"The canoe is much too slow to place in the top fifty," he maintained. "You know the start's important. It's all psy-chological. If you're near the front by the end of five miles, you'll probably remain there." Charlie slapped his bathtub of a canoe and grinned ruefully at me. "Of course, there's an exception to every rule.

"We'll start with one short pull, then three really long

strokes. Then we'll start our regular cadence, whatever
that is. Just paddle as hard and evenly as possible. When ei-
ther of us wants to switch sides, let's just yell 'switch.' "

Impatient to start, I nodded and shoved us off. For the
next hour and a half we did nothing but practice our first
three strokes. "At this rate, we'll need a year to get ready," I
speculated. Then we lengthened the start and sprinted the
half mile to the bottleneck at the bottom of Bassett Hospi-
tal.

Everything was going well. After a short lunch we pad-
dled leisurely the four miles to the Swamp. The water was
low, very low. Both of us gaped at the stumps above the
water. Paddling slowly along the narrow, winding river we
made mental notes on the locations of stumps, logs, and
rocks lying in irreverent ambush. At four o'clock when
Charlie suggested stopping, I readily concurred. I was feel-
ing surprisingly tired.

Lin, saying nothing, greeted the two of us with an
empty stare. Charlie apparently had promised to help his
wife that afternoon, moving and packing the largely un-
touched Payson possessions. Charlie shrugged, I kept
quiet, and the three of us ate a quiet dinner.

Fortunately, children often have an uncanny ability to
relieve adult tensions. As we went swimming later that eve-
ning, Johnny grabbed me and loudly decreed that we
would play "catapult."

Johnnie was one of the heaviest six-year-olds anyone
has seen. "Give him five more years and he'll play starting
tackle for the Green Bay Packers," a neighbor only half-
facetiously predicted. Wearing his intense, Churchillian
pout Johnnie pulled me to the pier's end and told me to take
both of his wrists and spin him around, flinging him into
the water. "It's all right, Uncle Herbie," he reassured me. I
looked over to his parents for guidance. They smiled wanly.
"Johnnie'll do anything new," Lin commented.

I stood on the dock's edge swinging, and then releasing
Johnnie into a wide arc. Each time he slammed into the
water all of us winced. But bubbling to the surface he raced

back to me, red-faced and without comment, and once more would grab my hands. Older brother Willie, not to be upstaged, implored his father to turn into a catapult. As Charlie lofted Willie for the umpteenth time he glanced at me. "How're feelin?" he asked. "Damn tired," I laughed.

As we headed back, a fisherman noticed the canoe on top of our car. "In the race?" he asked. We nodded and he watched his line slap the water. "It's low, lower than it's been for some time." He tugged at his slack line and then looked at us. "Good luck" he wished. A grin crept over his weathered face. "That's about all I can say. 'Cept I'm sure glad I'm not doing it."

For the second straight night I slept ten hours. When I woke up, Charlie had just left for his church offfice which he hoped to clean by lunch. Vinia, who had been waiting patiently for me to wake up, crept into my room at ten o'clock and pounced upon her unsuspecting uncle. A friendly fight ensued, in the middle of which I bellowed "Stop. Stop it. You've knocked out my tooth." Vinia was not to be denied a long-sought victory by being duped by a sympathy plea. "Oh, like sure" she yelled and pushed her foot into my innocent stomach.

Fully aroused, I threw her off and inspected my mouth. A small section of tooth lay upon the sheet and a surprised Vinia said, with a bit too much pride, "Gee, did I really do that?"

Looking up at me, a sudden realization flashed upon her face. "Herbie, what will your Cambridge women say when you tell them that some woman knocked your tooth out fighting in bed?" I concluded that Vinia had a pre-science somewhat beyond her years.

When I came down the next morning for breakfast I heard Charlie in the dining room. "I've got the paddles, my office, and the race, dear wife. "How can I be expected to pack?" Charlie looked at me. "Let's check out Unadilla," he suggested. I nodded, gulped down some V-8, and followed him to the car.

Unadilla is a deceptive former dam now marked by a

collection of rocks, broken clumps of cement, and rotting wood. From the top of the dam to the bottom of the fall is only three feet. But the current speeding through the rocks can quickly seize a canoe, shoot it through at a wrong angle, and force it to capsize.

The dam had a left and a right entrance. We decided to try the larger right opening. The current swept us towards the opening and suddenly we lost control, slamming against a large boulder, tailspinning our stern against another rock, and upending ingloriously. "Grab the canoe," Charlie yelled, but it dragged us fifty feet before drifting onto shore.

"We're going to try this again," I muttered. Wet and humbled we portaged the canoe over the dam and once more tried the right entrance. Once again we tipped. After five more attempts we wearily experimented with the left side. After two capsizings we threaded our way through the rocks, felt ourselves suspended in air, and then with a thunderous smack the bow crashed upon the water, burying itself. Miraculously re-emerging we sped full tilt down the river. "I guess we've got it," I grinned.

When we arrived home, Willie and Boogie ran up to us. "How many miles did you do today?" Willie inquired, half-expecting that as a warm-up for the race we had completed the whole course in record time. Calculating the eight approaches and portages to the dam Charlie looked thoughtful. " 'Bout half a mile, I reckon."

Willie surveyed our damp, muddy clothing, our bruises, and our cuts. He didn't say anything but turned away, undoubtedly wondering how he would square the results of the race with the advance build-ups he had been issuing to his friends for the past month. That afternoon I drove down to Otsego lake and practiced various strokes, but I surprised myself by feeling tired after the first half-hour. When I returned home, I fell asleep in the backyard and was awakened after several hours by Boogie's wet tongue.

"All this time," remembers Lin, "I had been getting a

sense that you tire very easily. I was really growing uncom-
fortable about your doing the race, and suspected that with
all the chemotherapy you might not have your former en-
durance. You seemed to be sleeping a lot, and taking rea-
sonable care not to overtire yourself. I mentioned this to
Charlie and told him I thought he should go easy, not worry
about the final results, not push you, and pretend that he
needed to slow down. Charlie wasn't enthusiastic. Like
you, he wanted to race."

The children, who had disliked playing second fiddle to
"a stupid old canoe race," were becoming excited by Mon-
day's world championship. Vinia pleaded for money to buy
extra film while Johnnie prepared detailed drawings of a
canoe with a concealed motor.

Early Sunday morning Lin squelched any final prac-
tices. "Charlie has to preach, not to mention pack. And our
best friends, the Olsons, have invited us to an old-fashioned
picnic." We looked at Lin. Her expression clearly indicated
that bargaining would prove fruitless.

As we packed, Charlie and I debated what food we
would carry in the canoe. Charlie mentally improvised a
banana-based drink that included strawberries, Tang, and
honey. "I'll unpack Lin's blender when she's not looking,"
he resolved.

Rural Cooperstown remains a throwback to an earlier
America. The farms, set in the Catskill foothills, usually
comprise less than two-hundred acres each and are run by
single families. Many of the farms perennially lose money
but somehow the families remain. "It's a good place to raise
a family," Mrs. Olson pointed out.

The Olsons' farm stands on rocky soil at the foot of a
hill. When we arrived early Sunday afternoon, various farm
wives were bustling from the old frame house with their
potluck contributions. Under the maple trees, farmers
dressed in white shirts and clean overalls smiled as their
wives continued to weigh the table down with food. Scam-

pering children descended upon Willie, John, and Vinia and dragged them off to inspect the cow barn. As introductions were made the farmers grinned shyly at Father Payson, probably recalling the times they had missed a service.

"You really one of those crazy kids doin' that race?" wondered an old, knobby-boned farmer as he studied me. "Yeah, but I'm not the only one," I grinned pointing to Charlie. "He's doing it too." The farmer looked curiously at my brother-in-law. "That so?" he asked, fumbling for an appropriate response. "Damn, damn, damn. I thought you church fellows could just walk on the water."

As we kept eating (I seized upon "You'll need it tomorrow" as my excuse), I looked around. Cows were grazing in the pastures. Mutts continually jumped upon John, whose delighted screams put any barking to shame. Occasionally a child would scoot up to the table, politely eat a hotdog and some potato salad, and then excuse himself to play with his friends. The relaxed dinner was a far cry from Cambridge and its school pressures, noise, pollution, chemotherapy, and crime (several people had been murdered recently on Harvard property). I fleetingly imagined that I had been placed in a time machine and was living in an America of forty years ago.

After playing a leisurely game of baseball, during which several of us tried to score a homer by hitting a cow, we settled down for freshly baked pies and vanilla ice cream. Mr. Olson looked towards the clear blue sky. "The river's low, really low. And it sure don't look like you'll be getting rain tonight."

Clutching a working model of a steam engine, Johnnie wandered through small groups of adults asking himself more than the adults, "How does it work, how does it work?" Vinia emerged from the barn, pouting that the cows refused to be milked. And Willie grabbed my arm. Proudly displaying me to his friends he announced, "That's my uncle and he's going to win tomorrow's race."

Finally the sun began to set. Lin and Charlie said good-

bye to families they had known well for the last four years
and the Olsons' kids *en masse* wrestled their steam engine
from Johnnie's octopus clutches.

Driving back, we stopped at a supermarket for coke and
granola for the race. Ratpackers from Athol had won two
sprints. A Ratpacker was purchasing twenty-six six-packs
for his fellow canoeists. "Gotta lotta contemplation to make
up for," he explained.

After Vinia, Willie, and John were called for bed, I
walked across Beaver Street past the nurses' building and
looked down Super Suicide hill to the Susquehanna. I
thought of the help that Claudia, Lin, Jane, Jon, and Debby
had given me. Without them I might not have completed
chemotherapy. And as I looked at the river I leaned against
a tree and remembered endlessly running along the
Charles, lifting weights with the blind weightlifter, hitting
the heavy bag, and playing squash the day after chemo-
therapy. The whole year had come down to this. "Tomor-
row," I vowed, "I'll be ready."

"Well, brother, it's your day at last."

Lin, who had risen at five to continue packing, now
stood in the doorway with a welcoming cup of coffee and
glass of V-8. Grunting reluctant thanks I flicked on the tape
recorder and sipped the coffee. It was six o'clock and not
yet light. I raised the curtain. Driving along Beaver Street
was a four-wheel drive with a pencil-thin Sawyer on its top.
"Today you die" I prophesied. As Linda Ronstadt sang "I
want to see what's never been seen, I want to live that age-
old dream," I slipped on blue jeans, a Dudley t-shirt, and a
baseball hat.

Charlie was busy with a tower of pancakes, totally
disregarding John's remonstrances. "If you eat too many,
you've got to go to the bathroom." Johnnie continued
laughing. "And they don't allow that in canoes." His laugh-
ter proved contagious; Willie and Vinia doubled over,
imagining Charlie and me in distress.

A few birds were chirping in the partially dark backyard
as several neighborhood kids saw us off. Cars and jeeps
jammed Main Street. At lakeside, we eased down our
eighty-pound Lincoln, ignoring amiable hypotheses about
its water-worthiness. Two women contestants dressed in
Bermuda shorts, sunglasses, and straw hats stared open-
mouthed at those competitors who must have graduated
from Charles Atlas University.

Stretched along the bank, canoeists conversed quietly in
anticipation as they secured spare paddles, life cushions,
bailers, and provisions. Girlfriends and wives snapped pic-
tures with their Instamatics, while little kids went from
canoe to canoe, silently comparing features and guessing
how well it and its occupants would fare. Somebody turned
up a car radio as the announcer predicted "beautiful
weather, temperature in the eighties with generally sunny
skies."

Ten minutes remained until the start. A line of ca-
noeists had formed around the park's only bathroom,
which was locked. As we stood around, a French Canadian
dashed up to the door. Cursing loudly he turned around
and looked reprovingly at us. He returned, lugging a large
sledge hammer. With Bastillian zeal we yelled with each
whack and then poured into the soon overcrowded hut.

What promised to be a bright sun was peeking over
Cooperstown's hills as we paddled to the starting line. The
mist was slowly rising. The temperature seemed to be in
the mid-fifties. We slipped into an empty space between
two Sawyer racers. Up and down the five-hundred-foot
starting rope, canoeists wore their full regalia—dark paint
under the eyes, baseball hats, wrist wraps, suntan lotion,
running suits, headbands, and old football jerseys. Two
canoeists had dressed as Indian chiefs. We had joined a
masquerade party for jocks.

The long line of one hundred thirty canoes filled up.
Canoeists nervously lapsed into self-assuring small talk.

I glanced ahead to the bottleneck created by Otsego

Lake contracting into the beginning of the Susquehanna. Spectators were spilling onto the river bank and disembodied shouts of encouragement floated across the still waters.

The first portage lay a mile downstream, shortly after the bottleneck. The portage, only eight feet high and a hundred feet long, should be easy. After that, the Swamp and then about fifteen miles before we would hit Goodyear Lake. Nodding my head, I knew that I was ready.

The starting rope covering the line of canoes stretched halfway across the lake. A powerboat with TV newsmen chugged parallel with us.

The starting official stood on the boat's stern. My muscles tightened. Looking straight ahead I quietly said to Charlie, "We're gonna jackrabbit this start." The gun cracked and we burst off the line.

One hundred thirty canoes can create a surprisingly choppy wake. We bounced around but stayed in the first third. I yelled delightedly and paddled faster towards the bottleneck.

"The whole scene was like something out of a Keystone Kops movie," Lin recalls. "Take a hundred-thirty canoes and jam them into the narrow mouth of a river. There were people going down the river backwards, hanging up on the edges, crashing into each other, etc. The funniest, of course, were the last boats. One couple hadn't yet learned how to paddle the canoe in a straight line and was merrily going down the river corkscrew fashion. 'Only seventy-one more miles to go,' a guy on shore yelled to them. Then there was the last couple of all—I got a picture of them— looking like perfectly normal canoeists until you notice they were going down the river backwards!"

As we neared the first portage, canoeists were already sprinting from their canoes, throwing them effortlessly over their heads and running over the road and down to the river. With a sinking feeling I knew that we were outclassed. But we leaped out, hurriedly yanked our canoe onto shore and ran like total idiots, despite the fact that we had seventy miles to go.

Resuming paddling, we heard yelling from the several hundred spectators lining the shore. We were still near the front of the pack. People howled with delight as they recognized their usually formal minister now squatting in an imitation birchbark canoe and wearing a pair of grease-spattered shorts, white t-shirt, and crumpled fishing cap.

In some respects, this was the most exciting section. The river was packed with adrenalin-pumped young canoeists striving mightily to pass everyone else. Canoes bounced off of or rammed each other. Canoes wobbled and capsized, while dunked canoeists ducked under the water to avoid boats bearing down upon them. One canoe, which nevertheless did finish the race, capsized three times in the first two miles.

After seeing us get through the bottleneck, Lin walked up Bassett's Hill. A group of neighborhood kids led by Dougie Wilson raced up, Lin later told me, "snowed by how smooth a job you did at the portage and screaming how many canoes you passed and how many were tipping."

I executed a strong bow draw stroke and we turned into the Swamp. Two capsized canoes lined the entranceway. Another canoe displayed a gaping hole from ramming a sunken log. We smugly swept past them and Charlie gave his first judgment. "We're doing well. Unbelievable, compared to last year."

We had learned the major trick of Swamp survival: anticipating and reacting in time to its intricate winding. The Swamp largely neutralized the advantage of speed. During the next half hour we kept passing hotdoggers, whose speed made them overshoot the turns, fail to spot submerged obstacles, or avoid getting entangled in the vines.

Suddenly a large, overhanging branch appeared. I threw myself over the prow and felt the branch brush my hat. In relief I looked back to see the canoe behind us capsize as the branch slammed the bowman in the chest.

We had cleared the Swamp. Now in open water, we paddled through a seven-mile quiet stretch. The early morning sun filtered through the leaves of the large willow trees which lined both banks of the still narrow river. In distinct contrast to the hectic jostling of the bottleneck and portage, the only sound came from the gentle chirping of the swallows as they swooped above us, flitting from tree to tree.

We were holding our own and even overtaking a few canoes. When we emerged from the willows, we heard fast running water ahead of us. I knelt down in the bow, threw an occasional bracing stroke, and smiled as we shot down the Susquehanna.

Halfway to Goodyear, we paddled on the flat water until the second portage. On the shore, a leathery old woman under a floppy hat shook a stick at somnambulant cows. We continued paddling. Heavy-set men rested beer cans on their paunches and smiled down upon us. Cars pulled off the highway as people stared at the winding chain of furiously paddling canoeists.

"Hey, you guys, don't you know it's supposed to hit the high eighties today? What the hell ya doin'?"

"Canoe race."

"No shit. How far?"

"Seventy-two miles."

"Oh."

We had reached Portlandville and on our right appeared the Twin Spruce campgrounds. Several dozen gray aluminum canoes from the last two days of racing were basking in the sun, like a group of beached whales. A stereo system bellowed out "Can't Get No Satisfaction." As we drew alongside the campgrounds, the Ratpacker from the supermarket stumbled out in his undershorts. Repulsed by alien sunlight he ducked inside and returned with a beer. He waved at us and yelled, "You're losing already." Exhausted by last night's contemplation, he collapsed onto the grass.

The race was widening out, with only one canoe visible ahead of us in the winding river and a couple behind us. I popped open a Coke, the only drink I would have during the race.

Turning to Charlie I yelled, "I wonder what Lin's doing?"

"Probably packing and wondering what type of fool she married," Charlie shouted back.

Lin, in fact, was worrying about us. "All that day, starting in the early morning, I had this strange feeling of impending doom. Not terribly disastrous, but not right. It was really wierd. I don't believe in the supernatural and maybe I should blame my feelings on the move. But I had this feeling that something was going to go wrong. It seemed terribly incongruous on such a lovely day, when everything otherwise seemed to be filled with such joy and promise."

The town names slipped by: Index, Hyde Park, Milford. I was exhilarated by our quick start and our regular sixty-five strokes per minute. Charlie yelled "switch" every eighth stroke. We had practiced switching from side to side for only the last two days but now we were doing fine. Sixty-five times a minute my arms pumped like a piston, thrusting the paddle out, catching, and then pulling the water back. "Sixty-five strokes a minute," I thought. "Let's see. In an hour that would be about four thousand strokes. Hey, for thirteen hours, that's over fifty thousand strokes!"

A few miles before Goodyear we sighted Lin and the kids waving from underneath an old stone bridge. We threw a brace turn and drew next to them. Willie, contentedly munching on a candy bar, appeared to be reflecting upon absurd adult rituals.

"How do you feel?" yelled Lin.

"Fine," I grinned broadly.

"Want some food?"

"No," I replied quickly lest Charlie decide otherwise. As we paddled away I looked back. Gazing at us with a placid smile, Willie continued to munch his candy bar.

As we approached Goodyear, our speed slackened. Each stroke seemed harder, thicker, as if we were paddling in a lake of slowly congealing cement. The lake seemed flat and interminable. We couldn't spot any other canoes to pace ourselves. The sun bounced off the lake and sweat quickly began trickling into my eyes and flowing down my nose. "Let's pick it up," I yelled to Charlie.

But Goodyear seemed elastic, stretching further as we continued to paddle. My crimson Dudley shirt felt heavy with sweat. I steadfastly refused to look up, concentrating instead on each individual stroke and then the switching. Before Memorial Day, the race had symbolized my resistance and endurance. Now, the only important thing was completing the next stroke.

We kept paddling. Muttering, "There must be life after Goodyear," I thought ahead to the white water at the foot of Goodyear dam and the fast water flowing down to West Davenport.

Finally I heard some distant shouting. Daring to look up, I noticed in the distance several hundred people lining both sides of the dam. With their handmade signs of encouragement, water coolers, Hibachi grills, and blaring radios, they thought the race was a festival. I shook my head and kept paddling.

Shouts in English and French marked the portage site. Twenty canoes were waiting to disembark. Suddenly I steered to the left of the waiting line. "What are ya doing?" yelled Charlie. Thinking that we would gain a few minutes I jumped over the bow, smiling smugly.

It's a strange feeling when one jumps into water and plunges straight down, rather than hitting an expected shallow bottom. I sank about twelve feet as my baseball hat floated to the surface. I bobbed up and two hundred spectators roared their approval.

"Hey, it's deep down there, fella."

"Degree of difficulty, nine point two" chortled another overweight, underbrained spectator.

I grabbed my hat and shouldered the canoe as the hoots continued. With Charlie pushing from behind we staggered up the muddy hill.

There was danger. Tired canoeists slipped on the mud. Cramped legs rebelled against supporting both a canoe and a person. Suddenly a canoe and a canoeist tumbled past me. The man crashed into a tree and then slowly rose to his feet. Contestants scrambled as the canoe bore down upon them and finally plunged into the Susquehanna. I pictured myself as Kirk Douglas scaling the sheer wall of a Norman castle as rocks and boiling oil rained down upon me.

Reaching the top of the portage, Charlie and I looked down upon the one-hundred-foot slope. To our right, canoeists were clutching plants, rocks, and other canoeists as they struggled up the hill. To our left, contestants had formed a slow moving line that wound past the dam, over some large rocks, and into the river.

As we joined the descent, two frustrated canoeists yanked their boat to the left. "Look out below," one yelled as he kicked his canoe down the moist slope. Bouncing over several small rises, the canoe miraculously evaded trees and grated to a halt on the rocks lining the bank. With a distinctly inhuman yell of triumph the two canoers ran madcap down the hill, grabbing trees for balance, and reached their canoe and the river before Charlie and I had taken ten steps down the hill.

Charlie and I looked at each other. Before the race we had vowed never to waste any time. "Let's get out of here," I now suggested. Dropping the Lincoln on the ground, we stepped out of the line. Bending over to guide the canoe we ran uncaringly down the hill. Suddenly I slipped on a soft patch and slid ten feet with the canoe. But I hastily got up and, quickly reaching the bottom, we stepped over a clump of rocks and re-entered the Susquehanna. We had been racing pell-mell for some five hours. We didn't know what place we were in. Yet we would continue this sprint until the sun set. "It's crazy," I decided. We jumped in and paddled furiously to catch three aluminum canoes ahead of us. We had fifty miles to go.

As we shot along we seemed to be one with the water. A rock would suddenly appear, we'd throw a draw, and speed by it. "We're moving as fast as the river," I thought.

But serious problems soon arose. The river's glare pushed an already hot temperature up another ten degrees. Blisters were growing and blood was dripping from the space between my thumb and index finger. And, in the early stages of hypothermia, or heat loss, I was shaking uncontrollably.

Without warning, the first professional canoes pulled alongside. Their sleek hulls, slicing effortlessly through the river, made a mockery of our own attempts. The pros had left an hour after us and, with fifty miles to go, they were already beating us. Suddenly I felt very tired.

Canoeists who had already surrendered helped raise my spirits. Eight miles from Goodyear, an AlumaCraft drifted slowly with the current. A ferocious pair of blood-dripping teeth adorned the bow while amidships had been written a red and black "JAWS." We drew closer as the two sunburnt, beer-guzzling occupants raised their cans in salute.

"We ran out of gas. Give 'em hell for us," yelled one while the other bellowed "Win it for the Gipper."

The current picked up speed and we hurtled along, faster than ever before. We were being drawn toward the rip. The canoe ahead of us misread the current and slammed against the river's wall. We threw a hard crossbow draw and as Charlie correctly read the rip we emerged unscathed. We slowed down. The Jensen racer, which probably cost six-hundred dollars a few months ago, was wrecked. The impact had crumpled its left stern. As the dripping canoeists stared forlornly at their boat the bowman yelled, "We're okay, I guess."

A few miles before West Davenport the current had become more leisurely. Up ahead was a small promontory where we would be making a sharp right turn. Dutifully, I threw my paddle out and started a draw. Without warning pain wrenched my back and gripped my shoulder. I lost control. Everything seemed blurry. Dropping the paddle I fell back into the canoe wincing with pain.

Charlie retrieved the paddle. "Let's stop," he offered.

"No," I angrily responded. Why had the pain come on such an easy stretch? Maybe the rip had caused it. "We're going to finish the race without stopping."

"Okay," Charlie decided, "we're stopping because I've got to take a leak." We beached the canoe, ran up the shore to a suitable bush, then sprinted back to the canoe. In our hurry we half-swamped it.

"How much further?" I yelled.

" 'Bout forty-five, I guess."

Pain was whacking the entire left side of my back. My left arm could hardly hold the paddle, much less stroke with it. I couldn't believe what had occurred. I had lifted weights for eight months. I had swum, boxed, and played squash. Never a back problem. But now, I wondered if I could paddle any longer.

I kept paddling. My head felt faint and I was coughing, presumably from hypothermia. Once again I felt bitter about not controlling my body. All the preparation seemed useless. And I resented our canoe. "We're paddling faster and probably just as hard as the other canoes," I thought. "But they weigh half as much. We'll never catch them." As we approached West Davenport two Sawyer Kevlars overtook us.

"What place do you think we're in?" I yelled back to Charlie. I felt like a fidgety child on a cross-country trip.

A long pause. "Don't know. Top third or so. We just can't move any faster."

The pain's growing intensity was making me feel numb and increasingly faint. "How're you doing?" grunted Charlie between strokes.

"Oh, just fine," I derisively replied. "I could do this all day."

"Probably will," answered Charlie.

The next seven miles was a winding stretch that de-
manded almost constant rapid draws and braces. The river
resembled an endless shimmering mirror. Sweat was pour-
ing off me and I was gulping or coughing each time I took a
stroke.

Should I stop? I've been practicing for the whole year
and now it's come down to this, I thought. The blister be-
tween my right thumb and index finger had ripped off,
leaving a painful red slash of skin. I glanced at two erst-
while canoeists sprawled on top of their canoe, drinking
beer, and waving to us. It seemed appealing.

Reading my mind, Charlie quietly said "Let's stop. You
don't look so good." If we did stop, it might only be for a few
minutes. A pause could help me. As I kept paddling I hur-
riedly searched for some reason to keep going and to finish
this race.

I thought of Claudia. I pictured her leaning across the
table, smiling at me and saying, "You can do anything you
want, Herb. But first, you've got to try." As I kept paddling,
I considered my Sisyphean attempts to finish chemo. I
thought of the vomiting, malaise, and my losing the thesis
in January. Now the race seemed like chemo, starting off
easily and then growing unbearable. But I had finished
chemo and the pride of finishing was greater than the tem-
porary pain and anguish. And as I thought about quitting I
thought of Loring, Jane, Jon and Norah, Debby and every-
one else who had stuck by me. "Just remember this, Herb,"
Jane had said. "Whenever you need me, just call. When-
ever." Giving up now would be letting them down. Sud-
denly there was no choice.

I half-turned to Charlie. "No," I shook my head. "We're
going to finish this race."

After fifteen minutes of hard paddling I still was shiver-
ing from the hypothermia but the pain had largely dissi-
pated, leaving only a dull ache.

As we approached Unadilla dam a string of seven ca-
noes was waiting to try the right approach. They apparently

hadn't noticed that three canoes had capsized just below the right entrance.

"The left's too small; we're all doing this one," a middle-aged canoeist gestured with his paddle. We disregarded his siren tempting. I braced a hard left to point us, just above the first boulder on the left. The current wrapped around us and we paddled furiously ahead. We grazed one large rock and flew into the opening. We hung in midair and then saw water surround us as our bow buried itself in the foot of the dam. But we popped right up and were swept along by the racing current. I looked back. Only a negligible amount of water lay in the canoe. Behind us, another canoe had capsized and the rest were belatedly heading towards the left entrance.

The river reached its lowest point and our canoe kept grating on the river's bottom. We would jump out, run with our Lincoln ten or fifteen feet, and then hop back in. We kept fighting the clock. Every several hundred feet we had to repeat the process. Twice more Charlie asked how I felt.

"Not so good," I replied. "But we're going to finish. Then I'll worry." Though by now it was four o'clock, the sun felt hotter than ever. As the miles slid by, we passed a mounting number of canoeists who had pulled onto the bank or had slackened their pace, hoping only to complete the trip before dark.

We saw an officials' stand at the Main Street bridge. "How're we doin'?" I yelled and heard in return, "The pros have just reached Bainbridge." We were at least two hours from the Bainbridge finish line and the race had already been won.

"It's the river; everyone's slow this year. But you're in the forties somewhere." The official paused to consult his charts. "And you're the first eighty-pounder we've seen. If there's a subdivision for clunkers then, hell, you're sure winning it."

By now, all thoughts focused on geography. Otego acquired the same geographical remoteness as Tasmania as we doggedly kept a pace of sixty strokes a minute. As a short stretch of white water thumped against our side I took a perverse pride in our clunker. Paddling it was a greater challenge than being whisked down river in a sleek racer. I thought of the line from *Alice In Wonderland* where Alice had to run twice as fast simply to stay in place.

"Seventy two miles!" I laughed aloud. "Why would anyone want to do this?"

But where were we? Somewhere near Oneonta, on-shore kibbitzers contributed to our uncertainty. "How many miles to Otego?" Charlie and I yelled in unison. A softball team peered up from a giant watermelon. "Five," they bellowed back. So we paddled for what seemed an hour. When we saw a family huddled around a barbecue, we wondered out loud about the metaphysical location of Otego. " 'Bout six. Maybe six and a half." So much for asking distances.

Lin had stopped packing by midafternoon. Along with a neighbor she and her children drove toward Bainbridge. Along the way they asked onlookers if they had sighted a fake birchbark canoe.

They reached us near Otego, thirty miles before the finish in Bainbridge. By now, the river was so low that we had trouble catching enough water. To compensate, we took faster and shorter strokes. Totally disregarding the propriety of a world's championship race, Vinia, Willie, and Johnnie waded out to us and laughingly yelled encouragement. We said nothing, thinking only of keeping a sixty-stroke pace and finishing quickly.

Charlie later recalled, "By sixty miles everyone was exhausted. But there was something really strange about you. Not talking, just sitting there. And not moving, except for paddling constantly. I talked to you a couple of times but I guess you didn't hear me." We kept paddling past pastel-colored houses half-hidden by pine trees and past cars which had pulled off Route 7 to watch us.

Oneonta dam was the third and final portage. Since it

comes after more than fifty miles and extends for three
hundred yards, most canoeists consider it as the most dif-
ficult portage. Charlie and I jumped out and hoisted the
canoe onto our shoulders. As we ran up the hill we passed
five other canoeists.

I pulled our Lincoln down the hill and down towards
the base of the dam. "You can't do that," Charlie shouted.
All other canoeists had been portaging their canoes for at
least another hundred yards before canoeing.

I looked at the water thunder from the sluice gate and
cascade over the boulders at the dam's base. "Yes, we can"
I replied. We pushed our canoe past several large rocks and
paddled furiously to the sluicegate. Suddenly caught in a
tremendous current, we slammed against a boulder and
pitched forward. We quickly sat up and shot down the river
as canoeists on the shore stared open-mouthed.

We knew we must be drawing close to Bainbridge but
the water seemed heavier with each additional mile. Blood
trickled from both hands. The back pain had retreated but I
was still coughing and shaking. As we continued to slide
past cabins and knots of spectators, I vaguely wondered
how I would feel after the race.

Finally around a bend I became conscious of the sights
and sounds of America—roller coasters, children munch-
ing cotton candy, smoke billowing from a thousand
chickens being barbecued, and public address systems an-
nouncing the latest lost children. Some four hundred yards
away the finish line stretched across the river.

"There it is," I yelled to Charlie. Sighting two more ca-
noes I sprinted furiously, disregarding solemn impreca-
tions from my stern that the race was over. I saw a Kevlar
and paddled faster. "Herb, do it yourself," Charlie grum-
bled. But he kept paddling and we caught the Kevlar as we
hit the finish line.

"From Cooperstown and Cambridge, Massachusetts,
Charles Payson and Herb Howe." The magic words we had
been waiting for since early morning. An apparently loud

round of applause followed and I fell back as Charlie paddled us up to the pier.

"Never seen a family canoe push as hard as you guys did," a couple of aides commented as they pulled us from the canoe. "You guys really burned in here." Since several finishers had collapsed on the pier or fallen into the water, the aides walked us to the shore.

Willie popped from the crowd. "You did it, you did it, you did it" he kept shouting as Charlie and I shook hands. We had finished in twelve hours, exceeding our goal by an hour. Last year we had finished in the nineties. This year we were in the low fifties, despite our canoe. We had done our best.

"Come on," Willie grabbed me. "You gotta get your award." As Charlie and I helped each other up the hill I turned to my partner. His eyes were halfclosed, his hair was an angry mess, and his shirt was stained with sweat. "I couldn't have gone one more mile," I said. Charlie simply nodded.

The Payson family and I sat down in the "chicken tent" for our complimentary chicken dinner. Suddenly I knew that I couldn't eat. My body was weak, uncontrollable. I felt as if I had just taken chemotherapy. The same awful metallic taste rinsed through my mouth. I began to breathe harder and harder. I couldn't seem to breathe enough.

I snatched a cup of coffee. Maybe the warmth and sugar would lessen the gasping. But my shaking hand couldn't hold the cup steady. To Vinia's amusement, the coffee sloshed onto the ground. I excused myself and stumbled down the hill overlooking the river. For some reason I was not yet finished with the race.

Along with the crowd I applauded the next few finishers. Suddenly my legs could no longer support me. I fell onto the ridge and looked out onto the river.

"We didn't win, we didn't win." It was a foolish statement but I kept repeating it to myself. An elderly, well-dressed man bent down and asked if I needed help. "No.

Thanks," I gasped. My mind flipped back to the chemo, to
Claudia, and all those hours spent in gyms or along the
Charles. A year had just ended.

I soon became delirious. The canoes stretched out on
the river now blurred and merged into one. I couldn't hear
any noises. I started to drool uncontrollably. Once I tried to
rise. But my arms buckled and I lay down upon my stom-
ach noisily gulping air and shaking from hypothermia.

"As we picked up the trophies," Lin recalls, "you were
really shivering but otherwise seemed okay. Then, after
you got your dinner you started getting worse and worse.
You tried to drink some coffee, but you couldn't. Then,
with considerable courtesy, you excused yourself and
walked down the hill. I stayed in the tent for a few minutes
and then went to look for you. You were lying face down in
the grass and shivering. You looked as if you were in pain,
but you said that you were okay. You were also gasping for
air. When you tried to get up, you couldn't."

Lin hurriedly fetched Charlie. After talking to me and
not receiving any response, they ran to the first-aid tent.
Two burly assistants half-dragged, half-carried me to the
first-aid station.

The emergency medical technicians were at a loss. My
vital signs were adequate but, as Lin remembers, "the
chemotherapy really threw them for a loss and there was
obviously something wrong with you. They called for an
ambulance. Just as it pulled out, Vinia appeared. I tried to
yell to her what was happening but she couldn't hear. Af-
terwards she told me that she felt as lonely and forsaken as
she'd ever felt in her life.

"All this time you, amidst your gasping, were very mat-
ter of fact with the technicians, telling them quite ra-
tionally about the chemotherapy and such. I've never rid-
den in an ambulance before. The whirling red lights, the
squawky radio contact with the hospital, and the medical
jargon that you kept giving the nurses about chemo—it all
seemed very lunatic and unreal to me."

The back of the ambulance swung open and I was rapidly wheeled into the emergency room. No doctors were present. Various RNs, LPNs, and aides flitted back and forth. Frowning, they listened to Lin describe my chemo protocol. Then they huddled in a corner, conversing among themselves. I heard myself gasping loudly, almost obscenely, for air. With my eyes and mouth wide open I imagined myself as a fish thrown up on the beach. The breathing grew louder. "Why doesn't somebody help me?" I wondered.

I fell unconscious for several minutes. When I awoke, an oxygen mask covered my mouth.

"Breathe deeply, in and out," a nurse ordered. She shifted my body, placing my legs higher than my head.

I breathed in; everything started spinning and appeared slightly out of focus. The nurses didn't seem to walk as much as bounce around the Emergency Room. I thought of the cancer, the chemotherapy, and my inability to influence the vomiting, chills, and diarrhea. I was now away from Cambridge but I still couldn't control my health.

The race's adrenalin had left and now I felt worse than during the race. "You were moaning, groaning, gasping, and shivering," Lin recalls. Every few minutes the nurses would drift over from other patients and appear miffed that I wasn't improving. I thought, "I'm in a hospital but I'm getting worse."

My toes felt as if they were frostbitten. I cried out, unable to tolerate the sharp pricking sensations. Lin wrapped several blankets around my feet and pressed them tightly to her. I kept inhaling oxygen and wondering why I wasn't improving.

Breathing heavily, I lay on the bench for almost two hours. Lin remembers, "You stopped talking and then started shaking like a leaf." The chills and pains were losing the ability to keep me awake. Everything was a blur and I idly wondered if I was actually going to die.

Suddenly, "This man's hyperventilating. What the *hell*

is going on here?" A doctor had finally arrived. "And what's he doing with this oxygen? And his legs! I can't believe this." The doctor angrily forced my legs back onto the bench. "Do you feel better?" he asked.

No answer. I was breathing too deeply.

"Stop gasping!" he commanded. I kept gasping.

"Look, damn it, you can stop it," he testily maintained.

I held my breath and prayed that I could stop gasping. But to no avail. I continued gasping.

Lin hastily described my protocol and the doctor's mood changed. He thought for a moment and then ordered ten units of Valium.

As I opened my mouth to complain that pills don't work on me, a crustaceous old nurse surreptitiously circled behind me. Tugging my underpants down, she thrust a needle into me. The pain was unbelievable.

My breathing soon subsided and I recognized the noses, eyes, and ears of the people who had been moving blurs during the previous two hours. I wearily tugged my shirt back on and glanced over at the doctor who was packing his bag. "Thanks," I said, "for a second I actually thought I was going to die." Not saying anything, the doctor finished packing, looked long and hard at the nurses, and left.

Charlie and Lin walked me to the car as Vinia and Willie pulled Johnnie away from a hospital apparatus that blinked and hummed. As I was falling asleep in the car Willie turned to me and grinned. "That was exciting, Herbie. Let's do it again next year."

# Nine

ON THE WEDNESDAY after I returned from Coop-
erstown, Dudley House staged its annual graduation din-
ner. I sat next to Dean Whitlock and, as he recounted the
year's events, I scanned the audience for my friends. Attired
in an absurdly floppy chef's hat, Ronnie lounged in a cor-
ner, smiling upon his three-hundred hungry guests.
Miriam and Jane sat at a table near the door. Whenever she
caught my eye, Jane would shake her fist in a victory sa-
lute. Jon and Norah had arrived with a red-faced Debby
who, three hours earlier, had passed her Ph.D. oral exami-
nation in Celtic literature. Bob, my former roommate, was
near the back of the dining hall. He had told me, "Back
when I saw you in chemotherapy I said 'Hey, that could be
me.' So I stayed away from you. But I was your friend and
staying away wasn't fair to you and well, I guess somehow I
was retreating from something inside me." Scattered
throughout the dining hall were students and Dudley
House athletes who had unknowingly created diversion
from the worries and physical pain of chemotherapy.

"As my final act this year," said Dean Whitlock, "I'm
presenting the Master's Award for Excellence to Herb
Howe . . . who has contributed unselfishly to this House." I
stood up, almost dropped the plaque, and found Debby

hugging me. Her face turned a miraculous shade of red as she exulted, "We did it, we did it. We sure damn did it, didn't we!" Jon and Norah, and Miriam and Jane were shoving their way towards me. When I had learned of my cancer, I had hesitated to seek their help. But friends had shoved their support on me and gradually I understood that I could retain independence while benefitting from their encouragement and concern. I grinned appreciatively as they gathered around. "I just want you to know," I began, "that I couldn't have made it without you." Straightfaced and wide-eyed, John looked at me. "Of course," he solemnly agreed. "Oh, crap," exclaimed Norah as she prodded Jon in the ribs. Then everyone broke out laughing as Jon extracted a six-pack from his briefcase. We corralled some more friends and walked into the clear spring night to celebrate.

The next morning I bounced into Conant's office. It was the first time I had seen him in three weeks.

Chemotherapy had pained and frustrated me. Yet those six months had given me a new confidence. My athletic schedule, labelled by friends as suicidal or macho-posturing, had shown that I could stretch my personal limits further than I had thought possible. Cancer had transformed my life into a sports analogy. As I ran faster and further, I realized that I could endure more chemotherapy. With the pride from having endured chemo I knew I could finish my thesis. As I entered Conant's office I thought, "If I've beaten chemo and cancer, what else can I do?"

Loring rose and shook my hand. "I hear from New York that you're bedeviling out-of-state doctors." As I sat in the familiar chair, he added "Everyone here thanks you for the vacation." I grinned and waited for the inevitable question.

"Are you continuing our chemotherapy treatments?"

I started to reply but Conant hurriedly continued. "You've completed the agreed-upon six months. That's good. They were the most crucial. Without them you might not be here."

He brushed back a comma of hair. "Both Dr. Grey and I suggest that you continue the treatments to the end of the year. Then we'd reassess the situation." Loring paused. "Basically, it's a case of 'the more the better.'"

Once again I was playing doctor. Usually when Loring had presented a choice I had agreed with his desire. But today I disagreed.

I told him that I hoped the surgery, radiation, and especially the chemo had cured me. Believing that, I couldn't submit to increased pain and possible genetic and cardiac damage. If, after all those treatments I still had cancer, then I assumed it was incurable. Given the choice of freedom or increased treatments, I would rather try and fail than not try at all.

Loring smiled ruefully. He had expected that decision.

"Since time is valuable," he finally asked, "what do you intend to do with it?"

We discussed some of my new interests, such as the hospice movement, writing, and working for the U.S. Senate. "Perhaps I'll return to teaching later," I told Loring. "But now I'd like to experiment with those things that have always interested me but that I've never done."

After we finished, Loring walked me outside. As we stood on the corner facing Elsie's I suddenly remembered waiting there ten months earlier. I had been angry, nervous, and afraid. Now with the aid of my friends, Dr. Conant, and other medical personnel, I felt as if I was beginning life again. Standing in the glaring Cambridge sun Loring and I shook hands. "Good luck," he wished. "We've been through a lot so keep in touch."

"I will."

A few months later I stood on top of a hill in western Massachusetts. Shortly I would attempt my first hang-gliding flight. From the ground, the hill appeared insignificant. But now I felt like an Apollo astronaut on the moon, trying to locate Washington.

Another novice started his run. He picked up speed and reached the hill's edge. But as he pushed off, the glider's nose shot downward. He crashed on the rocky hillside below us. The beautiful Rogallo aluminum frame was bent and the sail ripped. "My leg's broken," the gliderer screamed. "Get a doctor."

The instructor fixed his eyes on me. "Remember this, " he said, "either you control the glider or the glider controls you."

I snapped into the harness. "Go," barked the instructor. I hoisted the control bar, took a deep breath, and ran. The glider held the correct angle. I was approaching the edge. I ran faster. Suddenly my legs were running on air. I saw blue sky and heard the wind. I had a beautiful flight.

That afternoon I repeatedly lugged the glider up the hill, strapped myself in, and galloped furiously to the edge. Sometimes I flew and sometimes I crashed. The failures were more important since they made me work harder.

I was tired by four o'clock and would be happy with one more flight. Waiting for the wind to shift, another gliderer and I looked at the ground below. Pilots were disassembling their gliders as their friends rolled up blankets and put away coolers and barbecues.

I looked at my partner. "Life is like one long flight down this hill," he suggested. "If you work to do it well, you won't have any regrets when you've finished."

# Postscript

THREE YEARS HAVE PASSED since I finished my chemo treatments. Every six months I have X rays and blood tests. While six more years must pass before I am positively cleared of cancer, doctors assure me that I am probably cured.

Did sports cure me of cancer? A few years ago that idea would have seemed preposterous. Now, a small but growing number of medical specialists are actively exploring the relationship between sports and cancer.

Dr. Lloyd Schloen of the Sloan-Kettering Cancer Research Center points to a "growing body of evidence suggesting that cancer could be, in part, a psychosomatic illness." The leading proponents of a psychosomatic approach to cancer are Doctors Carl Simonton and Stephanie Matthews Simonton of the Cancer Counseling and Research Center of Forth Worth, Texas. They contend that stressful people contract cancer more often than calmer individuals and that cancer victims who manage to lower their stress through such devices as athletics or visualization stand a greater chance of cancer remission. In *Getting Well Again,* the Simontons write that emotional stress impairs our immunological systems which, along with hormonal imbalances, make the body incapable of combatting abnormal and—sometimes cancerous—cells. The Simontons' work builds upon an earlier hypothesis by the respected stress expert, Dr. Hans Selye, that emotional tension may produce adrenal exhaustion.

Could my running and canoeing have lowered the stress and supported my immunological system's struggle with cancer? Conant and other doctors discouraged strenuous exercise because no substantial medical evidence suggested sports as an anticancer agent. Indeed, the medical profession believed correctly that overly strenuous athletics could curtail a patient's ability to take chemo. My case was especially worrisome. A recent issue of *The Runner* magazine notes that "most patients on Adriamycin are too ill to begin an exercise program." Only in 1976—the year of my operation—did the Simontons seriously consider sports as cancer therapy. In that year they wrote, "To our knowledge, exercise has not previously been included in a cancer therapy regimen."*

Other authors have recently speculated about the connections between the mind and physical health. In *Optimism: The Biology of Hope* Lionel Tiger suggests that optimism improves our physiology. And in his recent best seller, *Anatomy of an Illness,* Norman Cousins describes the psychological and physical benefits gained from various placebos. Suggesting that "the human body is its own best apothecary," Cousins believes that a patient can transform hope into biochemical change.

The jury will probably remain out for a long time before deciding whether psychosomatic approaches can fight cancer. Yet sports for me played an undeniably important psychological role. By nudging me beyond my supposed limits, sports granted dignity and self-esteem when I needed them the most. As the blind weight lifter remarked about himself, "I needed something to make me feel less handicapped."

---

* Importantly, the Simontons prescribe their psychological approaches in conjunction with standard chemotherapy and radiation treatments.

Was my athletic approach to cancer of limited application? I don't think so. While a grandmother suffering through an advanced stage of cancer should not strap on a hang-glider, many patients with serious illnesses could benefit from sports. According to Doctor Paul K. Hamilton, a Denver oncologist, about half of all cancer patients can do mild exercise, such as walking, while about a third can jog, swim, or play tennis. Yet many of them don't and the reason, according to Doctor Hamilton, is usually more psychological than physical. Most cancer patients view themselves as frail and fear that exertion will cause additional harm. Numbed by their fears and entertaining a diminished opinion of their abilities, patients surrender their future to doctors, drugs, and machines.

The Presbyterian Medical Center in Denver has a cancer self-help program that actively encourages running for cancer patients. The program's director of counseling states that his athletic patients have "the need to take charge of their lives and not follow the crowd. In oncology, following the crowd usually means dying."

But sports is only one of the many ways a patient can assert his individuality during a time of suffering and self-doubt. The Simontons' description of athletic patients is just as apt for other patients who retain active interests. They are "more flexible in their thinking and beliefs, they tend to have an increased sense of self-sufficiency . . . improved self-acceptance, less tendency to blame others and less depression."

Some patients have taken up needlepoint, sculpture, or the piano while others have displayed a new-found concern about the relative growth of their tomato plants. Miss Marple took up carpentry and auto repair. A Massachusetts doctor described a middle-aged and overweight businessman who took up camping. Each week before chemo he drove to the Berkshire Mountains where he pitched his tent, gathered firewood, cooked for himself, and strolled through the pine forests. "He was performing something new and could assert a new independence," his doctor informed me. "The terrifying new environment of medical paraphernalia and fears of death as well as his dependence on medical technology didn't overwhelm him and turn him passive. That man's pride was more powerful than any drug. He lived but I don't think we saved him as much as he saved himself."

Before cancer I never seriously considered death. Such thoughts appeared maudlin and denied the optimism of life. "A free man," writes Spinoza, "thinks of death least of all things; and wisdom is a meditation not with death but of life." But cancer forced me to consider what I wanted from life and made me determined to achieve my new goals. Several years ago Betty Rollins, the NBC newswoman, had a cancerous breast removed. Now she pushes herself to new goals by asking:

> Am I doing
> What I'd want to be doing
> If I were dying?

I have continued my sports, adding scuba diving and parachuting. Before my present job as a southern African specialist I traveled to Africa, covering Nigeria and the war in Rhodesia for the *Philadelphia Inquirer*. I know that a lonely rogue cell may be hiding somewhere within my body, awaiting its moment to metastasize and spread. I realize that my very fallible body can limit many of my activities: ordinary aches and pains acquire a new meaning. But since conquering cancer I've placed a new value on life. Now I feel that I can control my life, which now appears as something given to each of us in trust. In return, we should not waste any of it.

Yet since I'm apparently cured, I worry about backsliding to a passively content life. Increasingly I've attached myself to people outside my generation. Starting with Miss Marple I believe that older people who are grappling with their fast approaching mortality can teach those of us who

still have time to benefit. Shortly after graduating from
Harvard I began volunteer work at an old-age home in
Washington. I quickly became good friends with an elderly
crippled woman. One afternoon we sat alone on a large
porch as she politely listened to my often bumbling at-
tempts at writing on Africa, parachuting, and carpentry.
She nodded as I spoke and then looked off at the woods.
For a long while she was silent. "I've never regretted doing
anything," she finally remarked, "but I damn well regret
that I haven't done more."